AF354140

A marijuana high can enhance core human mental abilities. It can help you to focus, to remember, to see new patterns, to imagine, to be creative, to introspect, to empathically understand others, and to come to deep insights. If you don't find this amazing you have lost your sense of wonder. Which, by the way, is something a high can bring back, too.

Library of Congress Cataloging-In-Publication Data
Marincolo, Sebastián 1969-
The Art of the High.
Your Guide to Using Cannabis for an Outstanding Life
p. cm. – (The Art of the High)

Includes biographical references.

ISBN 978-3-9817712-2-0

1. Cannabis 2. Consciousness 3. Mindfulness

First edition: December 2021
Eschborn, Germany
Publisher: Marincolo, Sebastián
Number of Pages: 248
First Printing: 2021

Summary: *The Art of the High* is a state-of-the-art minimalist guidebook teaching cannabis users to induce a high that can bring a whole bouquet of mind enhancements.

In memory of my father Andi Schulz,
1940-2021

With endless love and gratitude.

The Art of the High

Your Guide to Using Cannabis
for an Outstanding Life

by

Sebastián Marincolo

Contents

Cannabis, Animals and Evolution

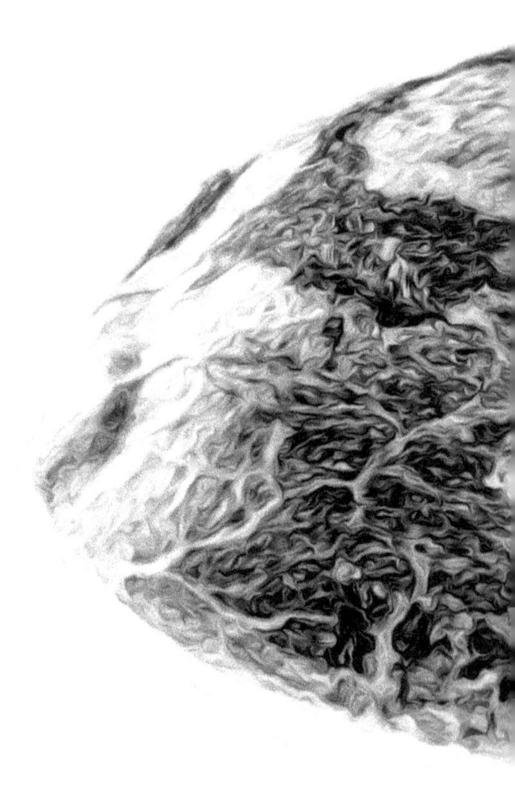

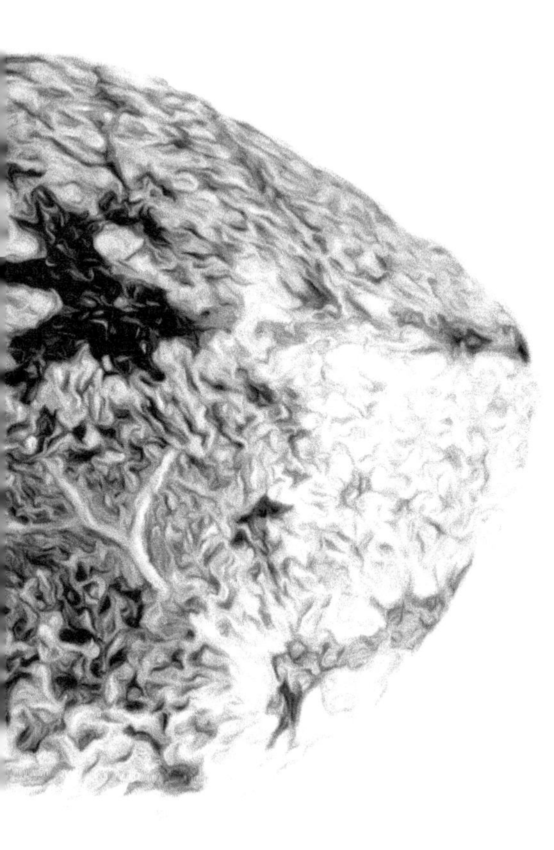

First Experiences

A cannabis high can relax us, focus our attention, and bring us into the here-and-now. The taste of maple syrup explodes on our tongues, seemingly in slow motion. We laugh as if we have never laughed before, endlessly, often without remembering why we started laughing in the first place.

But this is only the beginning.

Throughout history, millions of cannabis users have experienced effects like these. Only a fraction of them got to know the broad spectrum of the potential of a cannabis high. Many have opened the door to a new world, but they have never really entered into it.

If we want to start our journey into the high, we first need to know more about the cannabis plant, about plants in general, about the relationship between plants and animals, and especially between psychoactive plants and animals.

Cannabis and Evolution

The plant cannabis has evolved in two phases: the first of which began some 30 million years ago. In a second, much accelerated phase that started at least around 12,000 years to maybe even 1.75 million years ago, it co-evolved alongside us humans. For most of the time this was a loving and fruitful relationship for both sides.

Humans used cannabis for nutrition thanks to its balanced mix of fatty acids that seem to be perfectly geared toward our needs. We also used it for a whole range of medical purposes, as documented in our most ancient pharmacopeias, and we also produced our first ropes and paper with it.

We produced durable clothing and used the mind-enhancing and mood-altering properties of cannabis for inspiration, meditation, creative work, music, as an aphrodisiac for lovemaking, for celebrations, and other rituals in many different cultures throughout the world.

As a result of cultivation efforts, the plant became more diverse and was spread all over the planet by humans from its geographical origins in central Asia.

If we want to understand the cannabis plant and its effects on us better, we have to first take a look at its evolutionary history and those two phases.

The Endocannabinoid System

Let's go even further back in time: the success story of cannabinoid molecules in evolution starts long before the evolution of cannabis plants.

Cannabinoid receptor-like proteins can be found in still existing organisms that go way back in evolution, such as sea squirts. This means that animals started to build their own endogenous cannabinoids, the endocannabinoids, more than 600 million years ago, and long before the cannabis plant appeared on the evolutionary stage.

Today, these endocannabinoids can be found in all vertebrates and many non-vertebrates.

In the early 90s, some 20 years after the discovery of the endogenous opioid system, scientists discovered an endocannabinoid system (ECS) in animals and in the human body. Since then, thousands of scientific articles have appeared studying this system.

Like almost all other animal species, we humans produce endocannabinoids in the brain and in the body. The two most prominent ones are anandamide (AEA) and 2-arachidonoylglycerol (2-AG). We also have receptors detecting those endocannabinoids, the best known of these are called CB-1 and CB-2 receptors.

The endocannabinoids and their receptors together function as an endocannabinoid signaling system in our brain and body. It is responsible for a whole variety of cognitive and physiological functions.

The endocannabinoid system is probably our most important system maintaining homeostasis – the maintenance of a stable internal environment despite changes in the external environment.

The many functions of the endocannabinoid system include the control of functions of attention, learning, sensory perception, memory, sleep-wakefulness cycle, and many other important cognitive processes, as well as neurogenesis (the formation of new brain cells), appetite regulation, the regulation of mood, emotions, body temperature (thermoregulation), metabolism, stress, and pain. It also helps the body to withstand and repair damage and is involved in immune reactions and many other functions.

In recent times, scientists have come to believe the endocannabinoid system is embedded in an expanded signaling system in the brain called the endocannabinoidome.

The phytocannabinoids in cannabis have an effect on
this system because of their chemical similarity to endocannabinoids and can therefore systematically influence
and, under favorable conditions, enhance some of its
basic functions.

The worldwide success of cannabis as a plant certainly
has to do with the fact that the phytocannabinoids have
a directly influence on many of the functions of the
ECS.

There are hardly any endocannabinoid receptors in the brain stem, which controls vital functions such as our breathing and control of heart rate. On the other hand, you find many endogenous opioid receptors there. This is why an overdose of opioids can kill you by slowing or stopping your breathing, but on the other side, there is no single officially documented death from a cannabis overdose to date.

Clearly, then, we can see manifold therapeutic uses of cannabis as well as a whole bouquet of interesting effects on our consciousness during cannabis high because phytocannabinoids act on an endocannbinoid system involved in controlling all those functions.

The existence of the endocannabinoid system and its
many functions in our brain and body allows us to better understand why phytocannabinoids can have such
a broad spectrum of physiological effects on us. But if
we want to come to a deeper understanding how certain
varieties of cannabis can have different effects on us,
we have to better understand cannabis as a plant. And
in order to do this, we need to understand more about
plants in general.

The Intelligence of Plants

Cannabis, like other plants, has a highly complex bio-chemistry that has evolved over millions of years to serve many sophisticated functions.

Plants build a multitude of chemical substances to control various internal processes to interact intelligently and communicate with their environment.

In a forest, for instance, trees live in social communities: healthy adults nourish young shoots standing nearby with a nutrient solution through their roots whilst the young ones are too small to get enough sunlight from above. Similarly, adult trees can also help old and dying trees.

Plants produce various chemical compounds to protect
themselves from UV-light, drying, fungi, bacteria and
viruses. They make themselves inedible or poisonous to
attackers, reduce their fertility, or seduce them to eat and
spread their seeds.

Plants detect the kinds of insects attacking them and
react intelligently by producing powerful biochemical
attractants to attract other kinds of insects feeding on
the larvae of the attackers.

For millions of years, plants have co-existed with animals. They have developed fantastic abilities to biochemically affect animal nervous systems to influence their thinking, mood, perception and behavior. We underestimate cannabis because we underestimate plants in general.

Attack of the Ladybugs

In his seminal book "Intoxication. The Universal Drive for Mind-Altering Substances" the psychopharmacologist Ronald K. Siegel shares a story about ladybugs feeding on the Chayote Mexican squash.

When the ladybugs feed on the leaves of the squash they come in a group, quickly biting out a circular trench and leaving only a few narrow connections to then feed on the part in the middle. They have learned about the defensive mechanism of the squash, which detects the attack and reacts by pouring out a proteinase-inhibitor into its leaves. This compound blocks the ability of the ladybugs to digest the plant material. If attacked again, the squash pours out another hormone tripling the concentration of the proteinase-inhibitor.

But because of the strategic approach of the ladybugs, the squash cannot get enough of its chemical compounds into the cutout piece of the leaf, which is now only connected to the leaf with a few narrow bridges.

Ladybugs have also learned that the proteinase inhibitors are poured out by the plant to wide regions around their attack area, so after feeding on the leaf section they will fly around 20 feet away before attacking the next plant.

Animals and Psychoactive Plants

Ronald K. Siegel's research shows that animals of all kinds seek out plants that can temporarily alter their consciousness. Some types of ants live in symbiosis with a beetle that excretes a mind-altering substance; elephants systematically search for fermented fruit that contains alcohol to get drunk. Goats eat coffee berries to get excited and playful, American robins get intoxicated by eating berries known as "California holly".

A long time ago, Siberian shamans observed reindeer eat and trip on the psychedelic mushroom fly agaric (amanita muscaria) and drink the urine of another reindeer tripping. As we now know, the psychedelic gets metabolized in the liver and is better tolerated, retaining similar effects for the consumer in the excreted urine. A long time ago, shamans observed the behavior of reindeer and adopted it – they still use *fly agaric* in their rituals.

The symbolism of an Arctic Santa Clause riding a sled through the skies drawn by reindeer arguably goes back to Siberian shamans, who observed reindeer eating fly agaric to trip and then started brewing mushrooms for the same purpose. At the winter solstice, Siberian shamans would bring sacred mushrooms as presents to their people, sometimes having to enter the tents through fire openings on the top because deep snow blocked the entrances.

The Fourth Drive

Ronald Siegel goes on to argue on the basis of his extensive research into the behavior of many animal species that the use of psychoactive substances is so pertinent in the animal kingdom that we should see it as the fourth drive (the other three drives being for food, drink, and sex). Also, he argues convincingly, that humans copied the widespread use of psychoactive plants from observing animals.

The Many Advantages of Psychoactive Plants

But, why? From an evolutionary perspective, a reindeer standing tripping and drooling in the forest is more prone to being attacked and killed by a predator. How can it be advantageous for a species to trip on a mind-altering substance?

Could psychoactive plants help a species to survive despite bringing risks during intoxication?

Yes, and in many ways! Psychoactive plants can have many restoring effects on the body and mental health as well as other advantageous behavioral benefits. They can be anti-inflammatory, anti-fungicidal, aid digestion, and help to fight infections. Also, they can relieve stress, pain and anxiety; can help to get over traumatic experiences; to sleep better or to be more fearless in a territorial fight.

These plants may also be able to help animals overcome their rigid instinctive behavior to develop unusual problem-solving behavior that could promote the survival of a species.

Jaguars in the Amazon region, for instance, chew the bark of the *yaje* vine called *ayahuasca*, a strong psychedelic containing DMT. Local hunters use the substance to enhance their sensory perception visual acuity. For all we know, Jaguars may also use *yaje* to enhance their sense of smell while hunting.

Flying Carpets and Broomsticks

Cannabis produces hundreds of compounds to interact in various ways with its environment. Many of these substances bring useful medical effects for us and can also influence our psyche in many ways. Humans did not only observe the behavior of animals to then mimic their use of psychoactive plants. Thousands of years ago, they started to collect and breed psychoactive plants to better meet their manifold needs.

Just like the iconic image of Santa riding the sled through the skies, the iconic image of witches riding upon a broomstick once again incorporates the metaphor of flying, thereby indicating a visual trip.

In the Middle Ages, Northern European shamans already understood that psychoactive plants like henbane, mandrake, jimsonweed, deadly nightshade (Atropa belladonna) and (maybe) cannabis were better tolerated when absorbed through the skin. Women would "ride" ointment-laden broomsticks to come to orgasms and ecstatic trips, absorbing the substances through the mucus membranes of their genitals.

Likewise, the famous symbol of somebody sitting on a
flying carpet in a story of the Arabian folk tale collection One Thousand and One Nights probably goes back
to hashish users experiencing visual trips during a high
along with a feeling of weightlessness.

Hashish use was very widespread in the Arabian world
and is described in some tales of the One Thousand and
One Nights collection. The tales of flying carpets go
way back in history to the 13th century in Iran – a time
when cannabis use took hold in Islamic society there.

These iconic remnants give us a glimpse of the manifold
uses humans had for psychoactive substances throughout history.

Enhancing the Mind

Many ancient and modern cultures around the world used cannabis for various inspirational, religious, healing and other purposes, such as to induce sleep, states of trance, ecstasy, insight, as well as to enhance the experience of sexual pleasure.

My research concerning the cannabis high aims to come
to a deeper understanding of how cannabis can temporarily enhance our mental abilities to focus, to imagine
situations, to intensify all kinds of perceptions, to intensify our body perception, to revive long gone episodic
memories, to perceive new patterns, to introspect your
own minds, to empathically better understand others,
to come up with creative ideas as well as with deep and
meaningful insights.

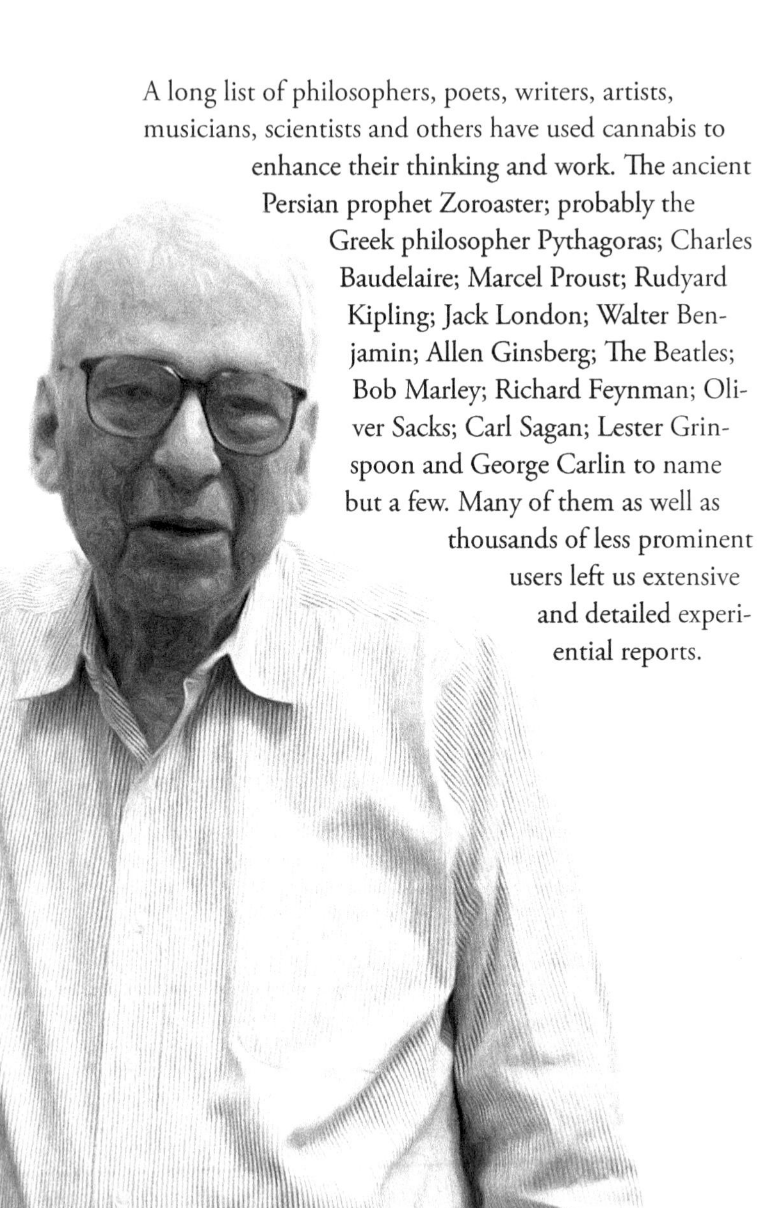

A long list of philosophers, poets, writers, artists, musicians, scientists and others have used cannabis to enhance their thinking and work. The ancient Persian prophet Zoroaster; probably the Greek philosopher Pythagoras; Charles Baudelaire; Marcel Proust; Rudyard Kipling; Jack London; Walter Benjamin; Allen Ginsberg; The Beatles; Bob Marley; Richard Feynman; Oliver Sacks; Carl Sagan; Lester Grinspoon and George Carlin to name but a few. Many of them as well as thousands of less prominent users left us extensive and detailed experiential reports.

The Fatal Consequences of Prohibition

The worldwide prohibition of cannabis started in the 19th century in various countries, mostly in colonies such as Egypt, Mauritius, British Guiana, South Africa (then the British Natal Colony) and Singapore, and spread to other countries and to the U.S. in the early 20th century.

In 1961, the United Nations' Single Convention on Narcotic drugs decreed *"The use of cannabis for other than medical and scientific purposes must be discontinued as soon as possible (…)".*

As a result, many cannabis users still do not know the multi-faceted mind-altering potential of cannabis. They have neither had access to good quality cannabis nor to fact-based information about its full potential. Our perception today is still affected by the aftermath of a worldwide propaganda campaign on behalf of a cannabis prohibition that has lasted for almost a century in most regions of the world.

As a culture, we forgot about the widespread religious, nutritional, industrial, medical, inspirational and other uses of cannabis and other psychoactive substances in human history. The prohibition of cannabis also had a catastrophic effect on science concerning cannabis and cannabinoids. Prohibitive regulations made scientific studies on cannabis and other substances almost impossible until just a few years ago.

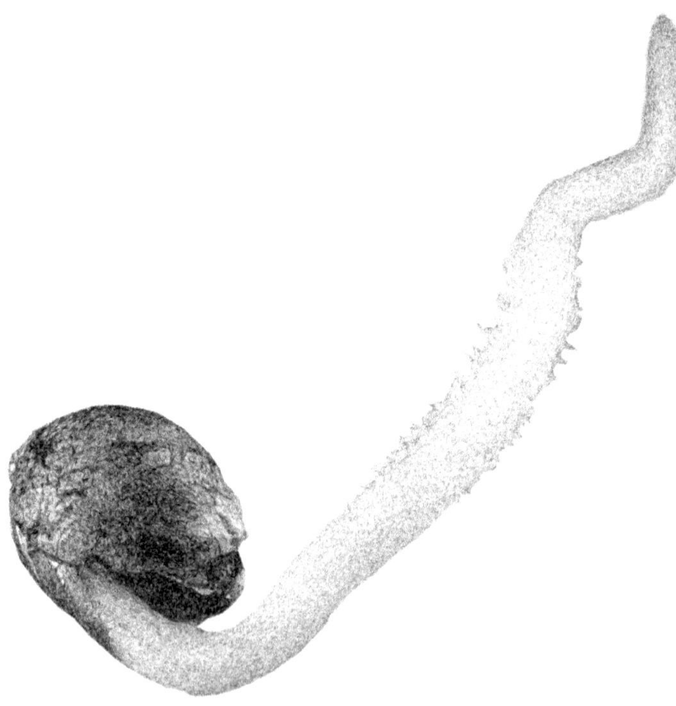

But the prohibition also had a deep and lasting impact on the most recent co-evolution of humans and cannabis.

As the prohibition became harsher under President Nixon in the 1970s, illegal cannabis growers in the US started to create new varieties optimized for illegal indoor production, where cannabis could more effectively be hidden from the authorities. These cannabis varieties were supposed to grow less tall, flower in a shorter period of time and produce a higher yield. Under this selective pressure, thousands of new hybrid cannabis varieties have been bred in the last decades.

More than 40 years ago, cannabis growers brought seeds
of a short-growing cannabis variety from Afghanistan
to California – a variety now known as 'Afghani #1'.
This variety contains high levels of the aromatic compound myrcene, a terpene that has a sedating effect in
combination with THC. Most hybrid varieties based on
the genetics of Afghani #1 have high levels of myrcene.
Afghani #1 was one of the most influential varieties used
to generate hybrid plants bringing a higher yield in a
short period of time without growing too tall.

As a consequence, however, many modern hybrid cannabis varieties have become more sedative and make it
harder for users to experience a high in which they are
able to benefit from various cognitive enhancements that
other, less sedative varieties can bring.

Dazed and Confused

On the illegal (black) market, cannabis users do not learn much about the nature of the plant substance they are consuming. Also, they usually only have access to inferior quality product; they do not know where their cannabis comes from and how it has been grown and treated. Often, they only get varieties of cannabis that tend to be more sedative.

Most illegal dealers as well as consumers do not store cannabis in their right conditions and expose it to pressure, light, heat and oxygen. This leads to the degradation of THCa (tetrahydrocannabinolic acid) to the cannabinoid CBNa (cannabinol acid), which turns into CBN when heated, as well as to the degradation of many other cannabinoids and terpenes. The result is the often-reported sedation and the confusing effect on the mind. Users tend to lose the thread in the middle of a conversation, to be disoriented and lost.

Many cannabis users only know this comfortable feeling of happy and confusing sedation during a high – and after many decades of prohibition, these users are looking exactly for those effects. They help them to relax, to forget about their problems, and to be happy during a high.

One of those consumers once remarked to me:

"The main point of smoking marijuana is to wreck me!"

After almost a century of prohibition and the well-known government disinformation campaigns against the so-called "evil drug" marijuana and other cannabis products, we tend to forget that cannabis products are sensitive plant products.

The prohibition of cannabis, then, has led to a dynamic
system in which badly informed consumers usually
only have access to the bad qualities of certain cannabis varieties which tend to be useful for a more sedative, euphoric experience. These users know nothing
else, so this is exactly what they are looking for. They
are actively seeking mostly the sedative and confusing
effects of bad quality cannabis to mentally relax, to help
them sleep, to reduce their anxiety, and to escape from
their problems.

The prohibition that still exists in most countries around the world adds another huge stress factor to the problems from which many want to run away and, thus, drives them to abuse cannabis even more for escapism.

In this situation, the use of cannabis can reinforce a kind of mental escapism that often leads to stagnation in the lives of users, rather than personal development.

Cannasseurs

The real 'cannasseurs' may also use cannabis to relax and for occasional mental escapes, but they do not abuse cannabis for constant escapism. They know their cannabis varieties and makes sure their products have been produced, cured, transported and stored in the right way. Cannabis flowers have to be kept in dark, airtight environments and at just the right temperature. This does not only preserve its aroma and taste – it is all about the quality of the cannabis high.

Indica, Sativa, Ruderalis?

These notions are commonly used to describe various genetic family types of cannabis. Indicas are said to come from the Indian subcontinent, Afghanistan, Tibet, Pakistan, and Nepal.

Sativas, on the other hand, are said to come from regions close to the equator, such as Thailand, Mexico, Jamaica, or South India. Cannabis ruderalis varieties are believed to have spread in the wild throughout Middle Europe and Russia, as well as in Central Asia and contain very little THC.

Many in the cannabis world believe that original "landrace" Sativas and their narrow, jagged leaves cause a
clear, euphoric, energetic high which does not affect the
body as much as other varieties. A landrace is a variety
of cannabis that evolved for many plant generations in a
certain regional natural environment, often under selective pressures of the local farmers who cultivated that
variety.

Various landrace varieties have been crossed in the last decades with the shorter growing indicas with broad leaves – the resulting hybrids flower faster and bring a higher yield. The psychoactive effects of landrace Indicas, however, are said to be different; they are supposed to affect the body more, often tend to be sedating, and make us feel "stoned" and "couch-locked".

Automatic, Auto, Ryder

Since the 70s, growers in California and later in the Netherlands have produced hybrids from landrace genetics they categorized as Indica or Sativa. These hybrids were mostly bred to be grown indoors because of the aforementioned prohibition. These cannabis genetics are photoperiodic, which means that they start flowering when autumn comes and the light gets less during the day. Indoor growers, therefore, have to first use an 18 / 6 hour light and darkness cycle for growth and then imitate artificial autumn by switching to a 12 /12 hour light and darkness cycle to trigger the flowering process.

More recently, growers have experimented with what they classify as Ruderalis genetics. It is not clear whether Ruderalis can be considered as its own species or subspecies of cannabis, but most researchers agree that we can consider it a genetic family with certain distinct features.

Cannabis Ruderalis had to adapt to rough circumstances and therefore has the ability to "automatically" go into the flowering stage without influence from a photoperiod. It contains only low quantities of THC. Indoor growers can just keep these hybrids with Ruderalis daily at 18 hours of light and these hybrids will go through a vegetative phase and then automatically enter a flower phase, as such they are considered to be easy for growers to handle.

These varieties are marked with 'Auto', 'Automatic' or 'Ryder' in their names. Some users feel that the high they produce tends to be more of what is usually said of the Indicas (body stone). This may change, as we will see new generations of hybrids coming up.

A New Taxonomy

Scientists like Mark Merlin and Robert Connell Clarke have criticized in the last years the often-used classification of cannabis in species of Indica, Sativa, and Ruderalis. On the basis of their genetic profiling of a wide array of samples, they suggested a new taxonomy with only one species of cannabis and several subspecies.

In their new classification, it would still make some sense to say that there are distinct subspecies of cannabis with the properties users and growers usually attribute to Sativas, Indicas, or Ruderalis.

However, there are three main problems that undermine the reliability of modern cannabis marketing that classifies cannabis varieties of Sativas, Indicas, Ruderalis and certain degrees of hybrids thereof:

- The recent history of hybridization

- The vanishing of landraces around the globe

- The lack of standardization in the cannabis industry

We will now shortly take a look at these problems.

The Recent History of Hybridization

Recent studies of modern varieties of cannabis show that after decades of interbreeding, statements about varieties being 70% Sativa and 30% Indica are usually meaningless when it comes to the real genetic profile of a variety. If you buy an alleged 70% Sativa, you may nevertheless experience effects that are more connected to what many users would attribute to an Indica. Also, you cannot tell anymore what effects a hybrid variety has by looking at the plant's morphology:

"One cannot in any way currently guess the biochemical content of a given Cannabis plant based on its height, branching, or leaf morphology. The degree of interbreeding/ hybridization is such that only a biochemical assay tells a potential consumer or scientist what is really in the plant."

Psychopharmacologist and cannabis specialist
Dr. Ethan B. Russo

Vanishing Landraces

The research of Robert Connell Clarke also shows
that even in remote places around the world, cannabis
varieties are not the old landraces anymore. Even in far
remote places in the Himalayas or elsewhere, many cannabis varieties you find today go back to the genetics of
Dutch breeders because illegal growers all over the world
obtained cannabis seeds from the Netherlands in the last
decades to grow them somewhere outdoors, hidden in
remote places for the prohibited market.

If you look for so-called pure landrace Indica or Sativa
cannabis plants today you may still get lucky and experience the typical qualities that are connected with these
types of cannabis, but it is definitely hard to find those
landraces.

*"Categorizing cannabis as either "Sativa" and "Indica" has
become an exercise in futility. Ubiquitous interbreeding and
hybridization render their distinction meaningless."*

Dr. John M. Partland, Cannabis expert

The Lack of Standardization

A "Jack Herer" cannabis variety coming from one seed company may be completely different to another one from a different source. Most of the production of cannabis for the legal market today is not regulated in a way that would guarantee that we obtain a certain stable genetic profile connected to a brand name like "Girl Scout Cookies".

Even in the medical cannabis industry, pharmaceutical companies that produce cannabis have sometimes switched their base genetics connected to a medical brand name.

Sadly, also, the medical industry focuses solely on THC and CBD contents and usually does not investigate enough other cannabinoids and terpenes that can affect the high.

How to Choose a Variety

If we want to benefit from a high that does not make us tired, dazed and confused many of us would prefer to get a variety that has the effects attributed to pure land-race sativa variety. However, as we have seen, we cannot simply rely on companies telling us about their genetics today.

But there are other ways to find a variety that works for us and there are many additional ways to make sure that we use it in a way that will deliver the best results. First, we need to take a closer look at the various substances in cannabis and what we know about their potential effects.

Synergistic Effects

Cannabis does not only contain the cannabinoid THC, but more than 140 other cannabinoids, over 200 terpenes, many flavonoids and other substances.

Many of these substances can influence the high. Cannabinoids, terpenes and flavonoids have synergistic effects – they can modulate, weaken and enhance each other's effects. Scientists, therefore, speak of a synergistic entourage or ensemble effect of a cannabis variety.

Many of the cannabinoids, terpenes and flavonoids in cannabis only occur in trace amounts. Therefore, it makes sense to look at a few select chemical compounds that often occur in higher amounts in cannabis varieties in more detail.

Cultivars and Chemovars

Varieties of cannabis or so-called cultivars have been cultivated in different environments to serve various purposes (to bring a higher yield; express higher quantities of THC; to have a shorter growth cycle, etc.).

As we have seen, however, many named cultivars today often vary in their actual chemical composition, depending on where you get them or under which conditions they are grown.

A more scientific classification of cannabis looks at quantities of cannabinoids, terpenes and other substances in cannabis varieties and classifies them into chemovars types – types of varieties containing similar substance profiles especially where ratios of the cannabinoids TCH and CBD are concerned.

Phytocannabinoids

The more than 140 cannabinoids in cannabis are odorless and have numerous physiological and psychological effects. They are present in the cannabis plant only in their acid forms and have to be heated and thereby decarboxylized to produce the typical medical effects and psychoactivity that patients and cannabis consumers know and value.

Delta 9-Tetrahydrocannabinol (Delta-9 THC or THC)

Like the endocannbinoid anandamide, THC acts as an agonist (activator) to both endocannabinoid receptors CB-1 and CB-2. THC is mainly responsible for the cannabis high.

THC is stimulating, euphoric, anxiolytic (anxiety-reducing), analgesic (pain reducing), a muscle relaxant, antispasmodic (suppressing muscle spasms), neuroprotective, antioxidant and has various other medical effects.

It can enhance various sensory and cognitive functions like vision, touch, hearing and attention, and is known to produce a clear and energetic high.

Note, however, that the effects of THC are biphasic, which means that they can cause opposite effects at different dosages. High doses of THC can therefore also lead to disorientation, anxiety, drowsiness or even panic.

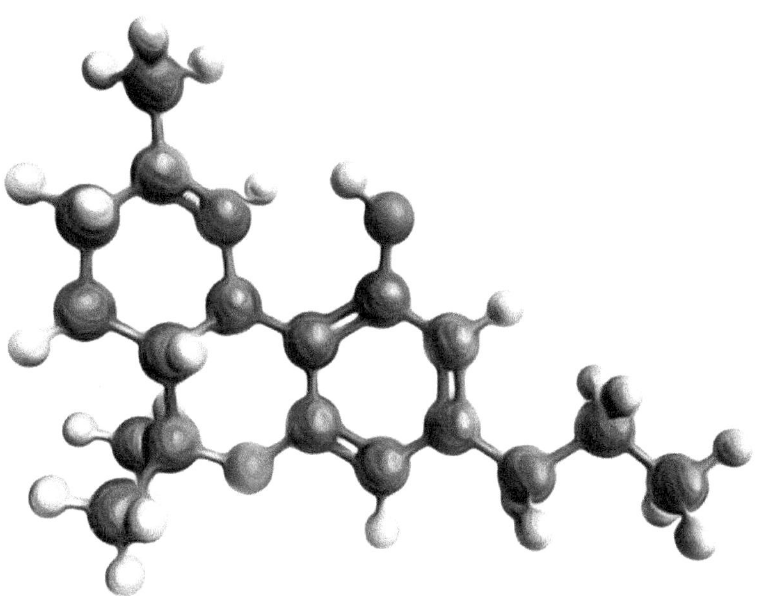

Cannabidiol (CBD)

CBD has some antagonistic effects on the endocannabinoid receptor CB-1, counteracting the partial agonist THC to some degree. Therefore, CBD can help us moderate some unwanted temporary effects of higher dosages of THC, such as paranoia and disorientation, as many users have reported.

CBD itself does not cause a high like THC. However, in connection with THC, it can also prolong the high because it slows down the breakdown process of THC in the liver.

Scientific studies indicate that CBD is analgesic, a neuroprotective antioxidant, anticonvulsive and has antifungal and antibiotic effects. It is also under investigation for its antipsychotic and anxiolytic effects and many other valuable medical properties.

CBD does not cause a high like THC, but it is to some degree psychoactive as it causes, amongst other things, analgesic effects.

Cannabinol (CBN)

Cannabinol is a degradation product of THCa, which comes from oxidization and is facilitated by heat and exposure to light. CBN itself is not psychoactive as THC, but in conjunction with THC and other cannabinoid and terpene degradation products in aged cannabis probably causes most of the often-reported sedation and disorientation. Importantly, then, if you want to have a clear high without getting too tired or confused, avoid CBN and other sedative degradation products.

CBN can be medically useful as an anticonvulsant and helps with pain or inflammation.

THCV-Tetrahydrocannabivarin

This cannabinoid is present mainly in varieties from South Africa and from other regions such as Pakistan and Afghanistan. Animal studies suggest that THCV may be helpful for decreasing appetite and up-regulating metabolism.

It is biphasic and seems to lead to temporary psychoactive effects only at higher doses. These effects last for a shorter time than those of THC. Some research suggests that THCV may reduce anxiety attacks, which would make it a very interesting component in a cannabis variety for users.

Anecdotal reports suggest that THCV in synergy with THC may have unique effects on the mind that still await further research and experimentation.

Delta-8-Tetrahydrocannabinol

According to some preliminary research, and experiential reports by consumers of Delta-8 THC products available in the U.S. suggest that this compound is the "lighter version" of Delta-9 THC with which it possibly shares a similar chemical structure. Reports also link a similar yet less potent effect profile concerning its psychoactive nature.

Products with Delta-8 THC began to boom around 2020 in the U.S. mainly because it had not been regulated as had Delta-9-THC. However, at this time the legal status of this compound on the federal level is unclear and may change in the near future.

Some experiential reports so far hint towards a more relaxing and "body high" effect than that of Delta-9 THC, but given the various products based on different extraction techniques. We should see this only a very preliminary observations. Delta-8 THC is definitely under-researched so far despite its promising effect profile.

Cannabigerol (CBG)

The plant uses CBG to synthesize all other cannabinoids, which is why some call CBG "The Mother of
Cannabinoids". It does not cause a high such as Delta-9
THC or Delta-8 THC, but could be psychoactive in so
far as it could possibly reduce anxiety.

Other Minor Cannabinoids

Cannabichromene (CBC) and its metabolite cannabicy-
clol (CBL) are only some of the interesting cannabinoids
that can potentially synergistically influence mental
processes like cognition, mood, memory and perception
during an altered state of consciousness.

Terpenes, Terpenoids, Flavonoids

Cannabis contains various terpenes and terpenoids, the products of naturally occurring chemical alterations of terpenes. These substances are aromatic compounds plants synthesize for many functions. They are involved in the plant's many direct and indirect defense mechanisms, such as antibiotic and anti-fungicidal effects, but they can also lure insects for pollination or attract carnivores or other organisms that feed on the herbivores or insects feeding on the plant.

In-vitro studies, animal studies and some human studies indicate that terpenes and terpenoids can have many therapeutic and psychoactive effects on humans: they can act as antidepressants, anxiolytic, help concentration and short-term memory. Also, they can be anti-inflammatory, antiviral, antioxidant, antiseptic, and may have many other therapeutic effects.

Flavonoids are known for providing yellow and other non-green pigments in plants, but also play various other functions in plants. They also have a whole range of therapeutic and other effects on animals when ingested including neuroprotective, anti-inflammatory and antibiotic properties, as shown in several animal models.

In what follows I will list and shortly describe some of the more important terpenes and flavonoids contained in cannabis varieties especially as it concerns their potential psychoactive effects based on preliminary animal studies. It should be noted, however, that the evidence on their potential psychoactive effects on humans is not very strong so far for most of them.

Terpenes

Beta-Myrcene

Aroma: Sweet, fruity, tropical, earthy
Effects, especially in synergy with THC: Sedating; sleep-inducing; muscle relaxant; pain relief; intensifies the effects of THC; probably to some degree responsible for the couch-lock effect of some cannabis varieties.

Plants: Myrcene can be found in mangos, thyme, hops and lemongrass. It is an important terpene to remember because it is the most common terpene found in cannabis and can make up to 50% or more of the terpene content in some cannabis varieties.

Delta-Limonene

Aroma: Sour; similar to citrus fruits
Effects: Refreshing; stimulating; anxiolytic.
Plants: Limonene can be found in citrus fruits, rosemary and peppermint.

Linalool

Aroma: Flowery, sweet, citrus fruits, candy
Effects: Sedating; anticonvulsive; anxiolytic
Plants: Linalool can be found in many plants including lavender, mint, citrus fruits and birches as well as in some mushrooms.

Beta-Caryophyllene

Aroma: Pepper, spicy, cloves, woody
Effects: Anti-inflammatory and analgesic. The only terpene that binds as an agonist to an endocannabinoid receptor, specifically CB-2, and is therefore also classified as a cannabinoid. The psychopharmacologist and cannabis researcher Ethan Russo believes that this is why smelling or eating pepper might help to relieve symptoms of anxiousness during a high.
Plants: Black pepper, cloves, cotton.

Alpha-Pinene

Aroma: Pine
Effects: Anti-inflammatory; bronchodilatory; acetyl-cholinesterase inhibitor. May counteract the short-term memory problems which cannabis users sometimes experience during a high.
Plants: Pine trees, conifers.

Terpineol

Aroma: Smell of Lilacs
Effects: Antibiotic; antioxidant; anti-tumor; relaxant/sedative; anti-inflammatory; antimalarial and anxiolytic. May contribute to the "couchlock" effect of some cannabis varieties

Flavonoids (from the Latin flavus, "yellow")

Apigenin

Color: Yellow

Plants: Parsley, celery, celeriac and chamomile tea

Effects: Antidepressant; antidiabetic; neuroprotective; muscle relaxing and sedating; anti-inflammatory; anti-oxidant; possibly cognition-enhancing; helping memory and learning. Also with a potential in the treatment or prevention of Alzheimer's

Kaempferol

Effects: Possibly anti-depressive
Plants: Apples, grapes, tomatoes, green tea, potatoes, onions, broccoli, Brussels sprouts, squash, cucumbers, lettuce, green beans, peaches, blackberries, raspberries and spinach

Boiling Cannabinoids, Terpenes, and Flavonoids

Cannabinoid acids, terpenes and flavonoids have to be heated and decarboxylized to be psychoactive. They each have different boiling points. Here are some examples:

Cannabinoids

THC	ca. 315 °F
CBD	ca. 320-356 °F
CBN	ca. 365 °F
THCV	ca. 428 °F

Terpenes

Beta-Caryophyllene	ca. 264 °F
Alpha-Pinene	ca. 311 °F
Humulene	ca. 388 °F

Flavonoids

Apigenin	ca. 352 °F

We need to know about how to heat cannabis products to be able to modulate a high. We will get back to this later in more detail.

Many cannabis variety names like Kush Mints, Gelonade, or Pineapple Express refer to a high quantity of certain terpenes which dictate their aroma, respectively. The names of these varieties may therefore give you some indication of its aroma and potential effect range.

However, the conditions under which cannabis varieties are grown often do not guarantee that the terpenes suggested as dominant really are contained in what we get as a consumer. Also, even if you get a batch of a variety called Super Lemon Haze that really contains higher quantities of limonene, we do not know yet for sure if this amount of limonene content significantly adds to this variety's anxiolytic or other effects.

Guided Trial and Error

So, let's sum up. How should we approach finding the right variety to get a high that can bring the mind enhancements we are looking for?

As we have seen, we have to be skeptical about marketing claims concerning the Sativa/Indica heritage of cannabis products and their alleged effects.

Generally, here are some things you can do to choose a variety to improve your high and adjust it to your needs:

- Try to find out how reliable the source is where your cannabis comes from

- If possible, get an exact chemical analysis of the cannabinoid/terpene/flavonoid profile of your cannabis product

- Use your eyes and nose to judge for yourself if your product is fresh

- Generally, look for cannabis varieties that are high in THC and contain lower amounts of CBD. Experiment if some amount of CBD helps you to balance your high

- The cannabinoid and terpene profile may give you a hint as to how a variety may affect your high, but do not rely on it too much.

- Bear in mind that not only are varieties of cannabis different but also that we as individuals are different in our reactions to certain substances. Gender, genetic makeup and other factors can make a difference. Some of us, for instance, may be more on the ADHD side and benefit from different substances to focus our attention.

- Experiment mindfully. Look out for varieties that deliver a high that suits your needs in certain situations – energetic, focused, anxiolytic, or maybe sleep-inducing or muscle relaxing. Remember: Only you have "privileged access" to your own mind while you are high. You know best how a variety works for you.

- Trust your own judgment more than you trust mar-

Personal Experimentation

Personal experimentation is the key to success when it comes to exploring the mind-enhancing potential of cannabis. In order to approach experimentation, we also need to understand that there are other important factors with which we can influence our high outside of choosing a certain cannabis variety. There are many different things we can do on our journey to improve our high, as we will see in the following chapters.

Experiment

Three Scents

Open an airtight box containing a variety of cannabis and smell it. Close your eyes. The scent of good quality cannabis flowers is usually very complex. Can you identify specific dominant aromas? Does your cannabis variety smell like lemons, oranges, like a pine tree, like moss in a wood, does it stink like a "skunk", or does the scent remind you of lavender, or perhaps candy? Try to identify at least three dominant aromas and note them down. Later, compare the scents you identified with the official description of the variety.

Repeat this during a moderate high. Can you discriminate and analyze the various scents better now?

Your Journey Begins

Factors Influencing our High

Imagine a young man living in Colorado in 1962 with a strict Catholic education and a firm conviction that smoking a joint will be his ticket to hell. Assume he is trying a joint for the first time under peer pressure somewhere on the street where he is afraid of being caught and sent straight to jail. No matter what the dosage is, he is likely to experience anxiety and more than likely will not enjoy the experience.

Obviously, an experienced, liberally educated, and open-minded adult who lives in Colorado in 2021 and decides to use cannabis for an evening of inspiration with his friends, listening to jazz and enjoying a great meal together will probably have a much better experience, even if he uses the same dosage of the same variety of cannabis as the young Catholic in 1962.

Dosage, Set and Setting

Our reactions to cannabis are highly individual and depend on the status of our endocannabinoid system and other factors. Especially inexperienced medical patients as well as inspirational users are well advised to *start low and go slow* when it comes to dosing.

We can learn a lot from the experience of others, but most importantly, we have to mindfully personally experiment to find out for ourselves which doses of cannabis can be useful for us in various situations. Some of us may prefer low doses to improve their attentional focus, whereas others may find higher doses resulting in a strong high useful to enhance their imagination or their love lives. Experienced users know how to dose their cannabis to arrive at various intensities of a high for different purposes. Remember that cannabis is often *biphasic* or even *multiphasic* in its dose-response curve and *bidirectional* in its effects. A lower dose of a cannabis variety, for instance, may help us to lose our anxiety and inhibition, whereas a stronger dose can lead to strong anxiety or even panic. We need to learn to find our "sweet spot" when it comes to dosing.

Generally, we should always remember that our high does not only depend on the dose and the variety of cannabis with its signature mix of varied natural psychoactive substances. Many other factors play a role in our experience of the high, or for that matter, any other altered state of consciousness: our convictions; mood; attitude and intentions (the so-called 'mind-set' or simply 'set'); our physical environment and the influence of other people present (the 'set-ting') during a high. The terms „set" and „setting" were introduced by Austrian biologist Ludwig Bertalanffy in 1958 and made famous by American psychologist and LSD researcher Timothy Leary.

If we want to benefit from a cannabis high we need to be aware and influence these factors to be able to better control our high.

Understanding the Risks

The use of psychoactive substances always comes with risks. Everybody who decides to use cannabis to get high should get informed about those risks – the more you know, the more you can minimize and avoid them. Careless and uninformed abuse of cannabis is one of the main reasons why many people have bad experiences when using the plant for psychoactive purposes.

In the last few decades, the dangers of cannabis consumption have often been wildly exaggerated. Sadly, our modern drug policies are deeply corrupt for various irrational reasons. For too long now, we have seen governments and institutions all over the world spreading disinformation about the alleged risks of cannabis use and the use of other psychoactive substances, usually based on self-produced myths and bad science.

Yet, clearly, there are some dangers associated with the use of cannabis and we should not underestimate them:

- Driving or operating machinery while high can lead
  to serious accidents and should be avoided

- Our blood pressure may temporarily drop during
  a high, which can cause dizziness and nausea or, in
  extreme cases, even cause one to lose consciousness

- Especially for inexperienced users, too high a dosage
  of cannabis can temporarily cause severe anxiety, disorientation and panic. Go low and slow. Dose carefully and slowly increase to the desired effect.

- It is important to know well and follow the law
  regarding cannabis use to avoid negative consequences
  for yourself and others

- Try to learn as much as possible about the cannabis
  product you want to use. On the illegal market there
  are many dangerous and sometimes very harmful con-
  taminations with pesticides and other substances

- Find out about possible interactions of cannabis with
  other medications – especially CBD can influence the
  effect of medications

- In terms of addictive potential, cannabis is nowhere near as dangerous as alcohol, but for some people it can still cause a psychological dependence

- Pay attention to yourself and your use, and involve friends and acquaintances in the process

- Adolescents and adults with less stable personalities and pre-existing mental health issues are at a higher risk of developing such addictions and may be more likely to experience negative side effects such as the anxiety and confusion mentioned above

- Learn what intensity of a high is still compatible with what activity responsibly. This highly depends on individual factors. For example, at a certain level of high, you may want to refrain from cooking yourself so as not to burn something because your sense of time gets messed up

People with a predisposition for schizophrenia or those who have already had problems with other forms of psychiatric disorders may be at risk when they use cannabis and should be especially careful with varieties high in THC and low in CBD.

Again, there is a lot of misinformation based on flawed studies out there on the dangers of cannabis allegedly causing schizophrenia or other forms of psychiatric disorders or symptoms, but some risks are real.

On the other side, many patients with psychiatric disorders seem to benefit from cannabis products – either from THC products or from CBD or from products with combinations of those cannabinoids, depending on their condition. Before contemplating the use of cannabis – for whatever purpose – patients with psychiatric disorders should consult a knowledgeable doctor for medical advice. A very good resource to evaluate the true risks of cannabis use is the website of the English psychiatrist and neuropharmacologist David Nutt: *http://drugscience.org.uk/drugs-info/cannabis/*

I highly recommend Nutt's well researched scientific information about many psychoactive substances including cannabis.

You can get high with a calm mind if you know the true risks of cannabis use – and if you know how to minimize and avoid them.

Baudelaire, Hashish, Set and Setting

Long before Leary wrote about "set and setting",
the great French writer and poet Charles Baudelaire
explained the importance of our environment and mood
for the experience of your high. He was the co-founder
of the "Club des Hashashins", a hashish club which
was formed around 1844 in Paris. The members of this
club included the writers Honoré de Balzac, Alexandre
Dumas, Victor Hugo, painter Eugène Delacroix and
many other influential writers and artists. They met frequently at a property they rented in Paris for their now
legendary experimentation with hashish.

The house was specially furnished with interiors created
to aid the experience of ingesting high dosages of hashish marmalade in an inspiring environment.

"(...) it is best to submit to its effects only in favorable environments and circumstances... Do not perform such an experiment on yourself if you have a bothersome piece of business to transact, if your mind is inclined to spleen, or if you have a bill to pay... As far as possible, you need a fine apartment or a fine landscape, a carefree and detached mind, a few accomplices whose intellectual temperament is close to yours, and a little music too, if possible."

Charles Baudelaire, 1821-1867

The Inclusion of Your High

If we want to set the stage for our high, we first have to learn how to include this altered state of consciousness into our lives. Just as we generally have to include and thereby embrace other altered states of consciousness, such as dreaming, trance, ecstasy or meditation as valuable states into our lives.

Altered States of Consciousness

We are not only rational, logical thinking beings in a state of wakefulness. Every day, we experience altered states of consciousness, with or without consuming psychoactive substances.
Our dreams are long visual trips, illogical, fragmentary, often bizarre and sometimes frightening.

We sit in a weird state of paralysis in front of our TVs, our computers, notepads or mobile phones, caught up and absorbed in a virtual world.

We get ecstatic dancing in a club or at a concert, or we fall into a trance watching a waterfall.

In our early childhood we swirl around and around like Sufi whirling dervishes to get dizzy, perhaps our first self-induced altered state of consciousness. Later in our lives, we will experience magical orgasms during sexual encounters which can seem to last for an eternity.

During extreme stress or fear, our perception radically narrows down to a tunnel, helping us to either fight or flee.

Altered states of consciousness are a part of our nature. They define who we are as human beings, enrich our lives and give our lives a deeper meaning – but only if we understand, value and include these states in our lives in a meaningful way.

An orgasm can be positively ecstatic when experienced
in a safe place with a beloved partner, but it can also be
dangerous if you experience it in the wild and when you
do not expect a lion to be sneaking up on you! You can
use your dreams as a basis for great paintings or for an
inspirational business idea, but you can also end your
life if you start dreaming while driving a car at speed on
the open road.

Life is a permanent endeavor to balance a whole variety
of different states of consciousness, such as dreams and
daydreams; ecstasy; orgasm; anxious alertness; con-
centrated absorption; rational thinking; trance; sleep
deprivation; a runner's high; meditation or states of
altered consciousness induced by various psychoactive
substances.

A cannabis high can enrich our lives magnificently once we have learned to meaningfully include this altered state of consciousness into our everyday lives – just like other altered states of consciousness. We all need an individual balance between various states of consciousness and we have to learn how to create this balance for ourselves. Some of us may need more ecstasy than others in our lives, others will prefer longer periods of meditation or being in a trance-like state.

If we want to stage our high, we have to learn how to choose the right time and the right environment for it. We also have to think about how often and for which types of activities we want to use this altered state of consciousness.

A high can bring various enhancements for many activities, such as experiencing art or nature; listening or composing music; surfing ocean waves; conversations with friends and family; creative work of all kinds; meditation; concentrating on a mathematical problem or having sex, to name but a few.

The more we understand the psychoactive potential of cannabis, the easier we can decide in the best ways we wish to use it – and even if we want to use it at all.

The First Time

As we have learned from many experiential reports, approximately half of users who have tried cannabis failed to get much of an effect for the first few times using cannabis. Many, such as my friend Lester Grinspoon who reported about his own experience, need to use cannabis three or four times or even more to experience a real high.

According to new scientific insights, several experts believe that some individuals need to be exposed to cannabis a few times first to sensitize their endocannabinoid system to build more endocannabinoid receptors, which then enables them to experience the full psychoactive effects of cannabis.

So, if your first time was a disappointment: that should not be a reason to give it up. Just like with sex, the first time may not be the real thing.

Importantly, however, this also means that if you do not feel much of an effect during the first sessions, do not go ahead and increase the dosage each time you try again. After a few times, your system might have built more receptors and then you could heavily overdose and get nauseous, have a bad trip or experience a panic attack.

You decide for yourself if you want to get high at all. And if you do want to get high, you decide when and how you get high. Choose your companion and environment carefully. Someone who already knows cannabis and whom you trust can be very helpful. Above all, you should know what types of use there are and how to dose safely.

Methods of Consumption

Various methods of consumption involve different types of materials – hashish, cannabis extracts, marijuana, dabs – which have been extracted, treated, cured or stored in different ways.

Methods of consumption like smoking a water pipe or a joint, or vaporizing marijuana involve different heating temperatures. As a result, different mixtures and quantities of a multitude of extracted cannabinoids and terpenes will end up in our body – resulting in a different effect on our mind.

Vaporizing

A vaporizer heats up the material between 280°F and 450°F, the cannabinoids and the terpenes evaporate without burning as they do in a joint, a bong or a pipe.

As mentioned earlier, cannabinoids and terpenes all have various boiling points. At a lower temperature, THC will already boil and evaporate into the air you inhale, while other cannabinoids and terpenes will only boil at higher temperatures. At higher temperatures, most of the substances in cannabis will have started to boil, but some may have been burnt already. Some modern vaporizers include a heating technology that heats cannabis at various boiling points to achieve a mix with the full range of activated cannabinoids, terpenes and flavonoids.

Vaporizing cannabis flowers brings many advantages over burning cannabis:

- Users often rate the high as clearer, less sedative and less confusing. The reason could be that fewer degradation products like CBN are produced

- The inhalation of the vapor is much healthier for the lungs than smoke and feels better.

- The aromatic experience is completely different; you can taste and experience the complexity of the full aromatic bouquet of this often underrated, delicious plant. To enjoy this better, use the mouth-to lung inhaling technique, first bring the vapor to your mouth, enjoy, and then inhale it deeper into your lungs. If you do not like the taste or want a stronger, more direct effect, use the direct lung inhalation technique.

- You can control which cannabinoids and terpenes you extract from a cannabis flower at a temperature of your choice, which makes a precision vaporizer a great instrument to experiment with.

- You can benefit from all the cannabinoids, terpenes and flavonoids present in a particular variety.

You can find many specialized cannabis vaporizers and vape pens available for cannabis extracts, dabs or other cannabis products.

Sadly, there have been fatal accidents with cannabis vape pen products from an unregulated market in the U.S. and other countries because some products turned out to contain substances that are highly toxic when heated and inhaled. If you consider vaporizing extracts, make sure your product is clean and safe. You need to understand exactly how your product has been extracted and processed in order to be able to know which mix of substances you get from it. Your temperature choice will depend on the type of product you have, as it needs to be melted.

Also, make sure that you can control dosing with your device.

When you vaporize cannabis flowers or other products, you will usually feel the effects within 1-10 minutes after inhalation depending on the dosage and selected temperature.

Usually, the onset of the effects is experienced not as quickly as with burned cannabis. Beginners should only take one hit of a 10-20% THC flower variety and then wait about 15 minutes. If you don't feel anything, try again after 15 minutes. If still nothing happens, wait a few hours or a day before trying again.

You can repeat this procedure for three or four days before increasing the dosage and trying two puffs. With a little more experience, you can then do the following experiment:

Experiment

Varying temperatures

Set your vaporizer to 280 °F. As a beginner, inhale the vape from good-quality cannabis variety without CBD only once or twice. Notice the complex herbal taste.

A few hours later, use a fresh sample of the same variety and set your vaporizer to 430 °F. Notice the more caramelized taste of your marijuana. Try another variety with a 1:1 ratio of THC and CBD and repeat this procedure.

If you are more experienced, you can use higher dosages. Can you discriminate between your highs resulting from the same variety at different temperatures?

Extracts and Dabs

There are many different ways to extract concentrates from cannabis. In the medical field, liquid extracts, also called „cannabis oils", are becoming more and more popular. These extracts are mixed with a plant oil to precisely blend the concentration and dosage. They have usually already been heated and thereby "activated", so they can be easily taken orally but they can also be vaporized.

Due to the high concentration and the slower onset of action after ingestion, it is more difficult for patients to gradually approach their desired dose. On the other hand, extracts have a longer effect than inhaled flowers and can often help patients with chronic pain, for example, to sleep through the night. Anyone wishing to use extracts for a high should seek further medical information on their safe dosage.

There are various ways to extract cannabinoid and terpene concentrates from cannabis. Depending on the method of extraction and on the consistency of the resulting material you get concentrates known as "wax", "shatter" (hard in consistency), budder, or other results. These are usually highly potent and contain between 60-90 % THC and other substances depending on the extraction methods.

Usually, tiny drops of these substances are then heated on a surface using a dab rig and the vapor is inhaled.

There are several downsides of dabbing. One inhalation of a heated dab may already be too intense for those with a low tolerance, so they might experience anxiousness; a loss of control; short-term memory disruptions for several hours; panic and other negative temporary side effects. It is generally hard to dose dabs and certainly not recommended for beginners.

In an untested dab there can be residues of unhealthy substances depending on the skills of those who extracted it.

Some users will choose to dab because it is a good method of getting a fast dosage of cannabinoids and terpenes in your body, which may for instance be very helpful for immediate and powerful pain relief.

Also, some experienced users report that dabbing delivers a strong, clear high, which may be due to the lack of degradation products like CBN which can often be found in dried cannabis products like flowers that have not been stored correctly.

Many users have learned how to dose their dabs well and prefer this method of consumption because compared to smoking, it is relatively easy on the lungs.

Those interested in dabbing should definitely insist on a reliable source for their dabs and make sure they understand how to get their dosages right.

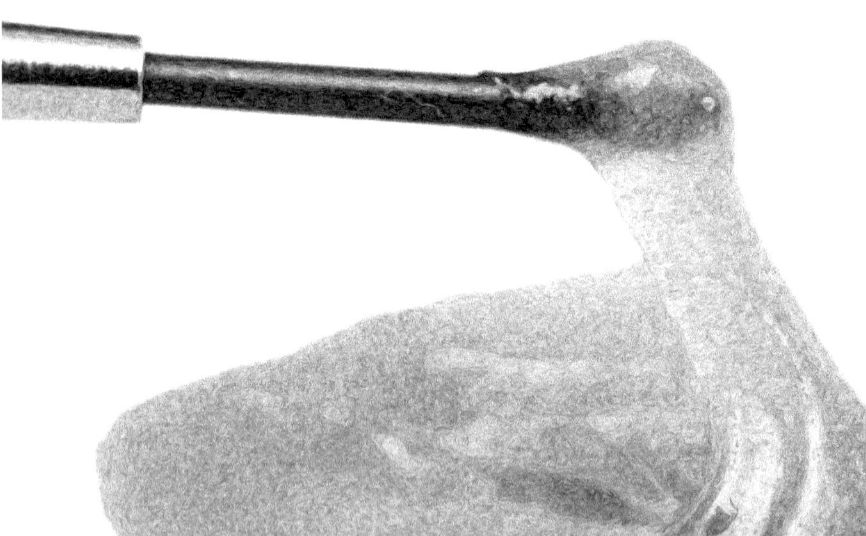

Smoking

We can smoke marijuana in various ways: in a pure joint; a joint mixed with tobacco; a blunt (marijuana in a tobacco leaf wrapper); in a bong, a pipe or, indeed, in many other ways. When we smoke marijuana or other cannabis products such as hashish, we burn the material at high temperatures of around 1000 °F or more. The resulting mix of cannabinoids and other substances is different from that of a vaporizer and contains some levels of the unhealthy substances like tar, which can cause damage to your respiratory system. The smoke from cannabis is presumably less toxic than whatever is produced by burning tobacco, but we still want to do our best to avoid it for health reasons.

A bong delivers the smoke cooler, which may be better for the lungs than hot smoke from a joint or pipe. It is unclear, however, whether it effectively filters out unhealthy substances to any significant degree. Dirty bongs or dirty bong water can bring further serious additional health risks. So, if you use a bong, make sure you always keep it extra clean.

Many users only have access to marijuana or hashish of a less superior quality, which tends to be more sedative. The nicotine in the tobacco sometimes helps to give them a kick and to stay awake and functional. This could maybe be described as "the poor man's way" to replace a great, uplifting high from a vaporizer or from higher quality edibles. It is like lacing a mediocre alcoholic beverage with juice or syrup to give it a sweeter and more agreeable taste.

The alcoholic cocktail, by the way, became popular during the alcohol prohibition in the United States, when the quality of alcohol became worse.

It is a myth that holding smoke in your lungs for longer causes a more intense high. More than 90% of the THC will be absorbed within three seconds in your lungs; keeping the smoke much longer will cause more damage to your lungs without giving you more psychoactive effects.

Eating and Drinking

Cannabis can be prepared in various ways to be effective in food or drinks. However, there are many things to keep in mind to make this experience a valuable one. To be activated for its psychoactive and many other effects, cannabis has to be heated and thereby decarboxylated – a chemical reaction that removes a carboxyl group from a molecule. For this you need to heat it to a temperature of around 250 °F. You should then add it to some fat before incorporating it into your food.

Before you prepare your own cannabis edibles, you should find a reliable source to teach you about the correct heating and preparation of food or even a drink, such as the traditional Indian bhang.

With the right dosage, set and setting you can experience a wonderful sustaining high, which gives you energy and permeates through the whole body.

Preparing food or drinks with cannabis is not for beginners. It is very hard to get the dosage right and, therefore, to avoid the danger of overdosing. Also, cannabis cookies or other cannabis edibles you can buy in stores may not always contain the advertised quantities of THC.

The full effect of the high can only be experienced between 30 minutes and two hours after consumption, and your high will last for a long time. Many consumers expect the effects much earlier, are disappointed after an hour, and then take more and overdose.

A strong overdose can lead to disorientation; depersonalization; nausea; a racing heart; panic and rather severe and potentially psychologically traumatizing horror trips. That is nothing to take lightly. So, be careful with your dosage and be patient!

When you ingest cannabis, THC is metabolized by the liver and converted to 11-hydroxy-THC. This metabolite can cross the blood-brain barrier more easily than THC and may cause an even more intense high. Research on this metabolite and its psychoactive effects is still very limited.

Therefore, if you ingest cannabis edibles or if you drink cannabis-infused drinks, you should be an experienced user. You should be in a safe environment, preferably with an easy option for you to fall asleep somewhere and ready to be high for a longer period of time.

Again, make sure you understand how to control your dosage. It is easier to find out about dosing for yourself with a vaporizer because you can experiment more easily and find the ideal dosage for you.

Note

If you consume cannabis orally, keeping food or an
extract or some other cannabis product in your mouth
for a longer time can make a big difference, because
THC then gets directly absorbed sublingually and
through other parts of your oral mucosa into your
bloodstream.

As a result, you may get much higher than
by just swallowing, and the high can
come on much sooner.

Also, it will make a difference if you
eat a meal before or after ingesting cannabis. If you eat before, the high will
usually come on slower than if you eat
afterwards.

When you eat cannabis, get your friends to
help you a little more and stay with you
while you experiment.

"What do I do when my love is away
(Does it worry you to be alone?)
How do I feel by the end of the day
(Are you sad because you're on your own?)

No, I get by with a little help from my friends
Mm, I get high with a little help from my friends
Mm, gonna try with a little help from my friends"

The Beatles, "With a little Help From My Friends"

Story

Hashish on New Year's Eve

At the age of 23 I was very inexperienced with cannabis, but decided to eat hashish chocolate pralines with some friends at a New Year's Eve party. I ate only half a praline and didn't feel anything even after an hour, so I shared a joint with some friends. After another 30 minutes, I still didn't get much of an effect from the praline and decided to eat the other half.

Another 30 minutes or so later a friend of mine came over and stared in my face, amazed, and said that he had never seen a face turning green like that!

I felt as if somebody had glued me to my chair, I felt almost catatonic, and observed another friend who had ingested a praline raiding the buffet. My right ear started to itch, so I tried to scratch it, but that didn't bring any relief. I turned my head and watched my hand making scratching movements somewhere in the air one-foot away from my head. I felt nauseous.

A friend came over to bring me a coffee and said it would help, but I did not drink it because I had a hard time holding the coffee without spilling it. Moving the cup to my mouth felt like an impos-   sible mission. Also, I became paranoid and wondered if somebody had managed to put more hashish into the coffee.

An hour later, another friend helped me to walk down a stairway. I looked down, trying hard to coordinate my leg movements. Every time I looked up I was convinced I was at a different location in the city, or even in a different city entirely. Every few seconds I had this feeling of total confusion we sometimes experience when we travel to a different country, wake up in the first morning in a hotel room and for a few seconds fail to grasp where we actually are.

My mind was completely fragmented. I had some moments of clarity and my friend and I laughed a lot about my ridiculous condition, but for a long time I went through fears and a state of helplessness that I wouldn't want others to experience.

Topical Application

Medicinally, cannabis products can also produce various beneficial effects on the skin. Topical medicinal uses of cannabis were described more than 3,500 years ago in the Egyptian pharmacopeia Papyrus Eber and in other ancient pharmacopeias around the world. Several years ago, physicians once again began recommending cannabis suppositories or other cannabis products for various purposes such as endometriosis, pelvic and rectal pain or PMS.

As far as the mind-altering aspect of cannabis is concerned, vaginal and anal applications have become particularly interesting for many users.

For some years now, companies in the USA have been producing cannabis products that are intended to enrich the sexual experience when used vaginally, for example.

Some of the women who used those cannabis products or self-made products topically in this way reported, among other things, that they actually had a more intense orgasm, they felt more relaxed and felt less pain and more pleasure during intercourse. Some reported that they had an orgasm for the first time ever, in one case, this was after having been sexually traumatized at an early age before.

However, other women also reported problems with vaginal dryness, which can apparently be influenced by the choice of varieties.

While many women do not feel any psychoactive effect from this form of application, some report an intensely experienced high from vaginal application, which some say has positively influenced their sex life in many ways, but sometimes also negatively. We will take a look at the subject of the cannabis high and lovemaking later in more detail.

As far as dosage is concerned, it is very important to start with a low dose and increase it slowly when using this form of application. Even with legal, standardized cannabis products available in some countries today, it is difficult to give exact information here.

How to Avoid a Difficult Trip

- Before you use cannabis for the first time, talk to experienced users about dosage; set and setting and the varieties of cannabis available and their typical effects.

- Do not get high on an empty stomach and keep something sweet, healthy and delicious to eat at hand. A high can lead to low blood pressure or lower blood sugar levels and can make your heart race. Also, make sure you are hydrated.

- Enjoy your high in a great environment with caring friends or family. Designate a friend to take care of you if you take higher dosages.

- For the first few times, you should be close to a place where you can easily retreat, relax and fall asleep if necessary.

- Start low and go slow. Start with a low dose and do not increase the dose the first few times you are using cannabis if you do not feel much of an effect.

- Do not get high as a beginner if you are in a bad mood or if there is something in your vicinity or on your mind which could distress or upset you, unless you are a cannabis patient receiving treatment and your doctor has advised you to take cannabis for depression or anxiety

- If available, start using a variety that is said to be euphoric and uplifting

- Make your experiences using a vaping method first. Keep aside ingesting cannabis products or dabbing for later when you are more experienced.

How to Get Through a Difficult Trip

- Seek a safe and calm space and sit down somewhere comfortably. Breathe calmly. Feel the energy that comes through breathing.

- Remember: even a strong overdose of marijuana is not deadly, although the temporary effects on your mind can be really strong. Nobody has ever died from a marijuana overdose.

- If possible, ask a friend to take care of you. They should first help to move you to a relaxing, comfortable environment.

- Concentrate on something inspiring and beautiful. Relax with some music, enjoy watching art, something natural like a landscape, or a funny movie. Get a hug from a good friend and feel their presence. Breathe calmly.

- Remember: you will come down and feel better after a while. All this is temporary.

- If you feel cold, weak and dizzy, get a blanket or put another layer of clothing on. Eat or drink something sweet to get your blood sugar level up. This can also help reduce your heart rate racing.

- Drink water or juice, stay hydrated, and eat something pleasant to get your blood sugar up.

- Try smelling ground pepper or even chew on some peppercorns. This may help reduce anxiety. The terpene beta-Caryophyllene present in pepper acts on the endocannabinoid receptor CB-2 in our body and modulates the effects of THC, resulting in a calming, anxiolytic effect.

- Try CBD flowers in a vaporizer with almost no THC, or use a full spectrum CBD extract. CBD may help you to come down.

Note

Even a high causing strong fears or panic can have a great value for your life. Sometimes we focus on strong, existential fears or on some problems in our lives, and they overwhelm us. This confrontation can be painful, but often we can make progress by thinking about issues during these intense highs.

If you still want to avoid negative thoughts during a high, then try to direct your attention to something beautiful, calm, inspiring.

I've gotten into the habit of mindfully observing myself whenever I'm on a high, so I notice when I get stuck on negative thoughts, for example. If I don't want to follow that, I clap my hands once and say,

„Go away, bad thought."

Then, I turn my attention to something else.

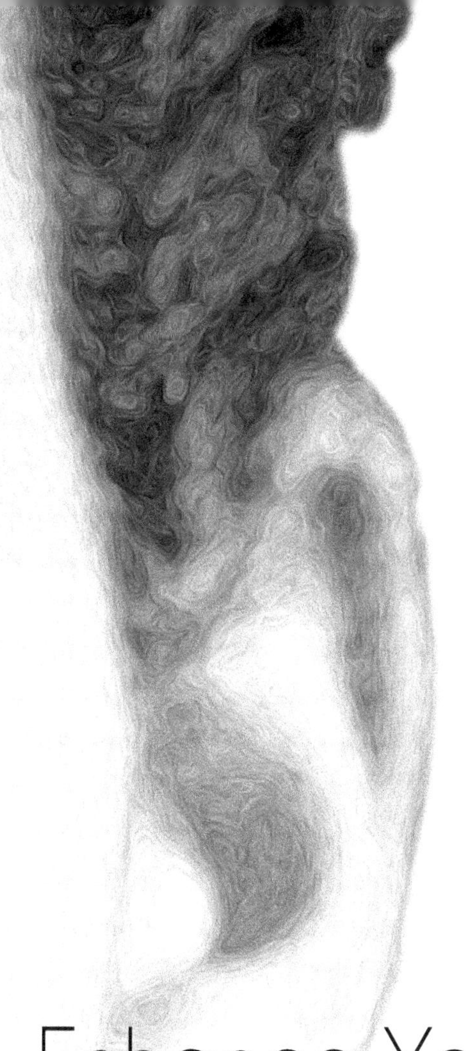

Enhance Your Mind

The Enhancement Potential of the High

Cannabis has a wide range of diverse effects on our mind, but there are certainly some typical effects on our perception and thought processes. If you know what these typical effects are and learn how to deal with them, you can utilize the full potential of a cannabis high. In what follows I will introduce some of the most important effects and describe some experiments to help you appreciate these enhancements better.

Try to find a variety of cannabis that does not make you feel tired and which you feel does not disturb your short-term memory too much. Use a vaporizer at a lower temperature to produce a clear, uplifting and energizing high. Or whatever you find useful for yourself.

If you want to become a cannasseur, you should experiment in order to get to know how certain varieties, quantities and various methods of application produce the best effects for you.

Cherish Your High

It's important that you change your attitude towards these altered states of consciousness. It doesn't matter if you use your high only to relax, or to sleep; to alleviate pain, or to enhance your creativity or love life. Once you understand that it can be useful to you in some sense, you can overcome prejudices and shame and embrace it as something valuable.

Take Notes

Get a simple notebook as a 'high diary' and keep it close by to where you get high. Write down short notes about remarkable impressions, observations and memories or ideas during your high. You do not have to spell them out exactly word by word. Usually, you will remember more details of your observations by looking at your notes at a later time.

Take a Tolerance Break

If you are a daily or very frequent user of cannabis and have developed a tolerance, you should take a tolerance break of at least a week before you start with the following exercises.

A Bouquet of Mental Enhancements

Throughout history, cannabis users have reported a whole variety of temporary perceptual and mind enhancements during a high. I have analyzed hundreds of detailed and mostly independent reports of users worldwide, which variously describe:

- The feeling of awe

- An intensification of sensory experiences

- A focusing effect on attention

- A strong perception of the "here-and-now"

- More acuteness and detail in perception

- A better ability to remember past episodes

- The enhancement of imagination

- "Mind racing" – rapid associative thinking

- Mood modulation

- The slowdown of time perception

- An intensification of bodily sensations

- Heightened creativity

- An enhanced sense of humor

- An enhanced ability to introspection and understanding oneself

- Enhanced empathic understanding

- Deep, spontaneous insights

The Feeling of Awe

Aristotle believed that awe and astonishment are the beginning of all philosophy. During a high we often experience a strong feeling of awe; we are amazed at the sound of a waterfall as if we were hearing it for the first time.

We become hyperfocused, our sensations seem intensified, and we marvel at the details and the beauty of what we see, hear, smell, taste, or touch.

Many things appear as if we would see them for the first time: fresh; intense; colorful and in breathtaking detail. Time seems to stand still as the feeling of awe overwhelms us. This feeling of awe can spark our curiosity and we start to re-examine the nature of things around us. A high can make us a start a new, curious quest for knowledge. My friend Jason Silva often emphasizes the importance of this feeling of awe during a high and I fully agree with him that this is one of the most wonderful and useful enhancements that a high can bring.

„*The most beautiful thing we can experience is mystery. It is the basic feeling that stands at the cradle of true art and science. He who does not know it and can no longer wonder, no longer marvel, is, so to speak, dead and his eye extinguished.*“

Albert Einstein

Before you get high, reflect on your attitude. If you want to get high playing a computer game, you will probably enhance the intensity of the experience and fun. Is this all you want?

Your attitude makes a difference. If you want your high to be a journey that takes you to really new places, choose your environment. Maybe you want to take a look at a painting and see it in a new light; or listen to music you would usually not listen to, like classical music or Indian sitar music, or maybe just experience nature in a new way.

The First Time, Once Again

When you are high, note the intensity with which you perceive various well-known situations. How does a kiss feel now? How does it feel to gaze at the moon and the stars in a clear night sky? If you have the feeling that you experience something as intense as if for the first time, take short notes describing your experience.

Focusing Your Attention

A high can strongly focus our selective attention; we focus on the taste of wine and discover new nuances to it. We focus intensely on a movie and can then appreciate the acting more, or suddenly understand how well the soundtrack expresses the emotional world of the story's protagonists. Or we focus on a friend's facial expression when they tell us a story, and we suddenly understand better how deeply happy they are watching their smile. We can also use this stronger focus of attention during a high to turn our gaze inward and to strongly concentrate on our own imagination, memories or thoughts.

We can also use this stronger focus of attention during a high to turn our gaze inward and to strongly concentrate on our own imagination, memories or thoughts.

Experiment

Focus on the Instruments

When listening to a song while high, try to concentrate selectively on the separate instruments. Focus on the drumming for a while. Then, focus on the bass, then focus on the vocals and then focus on how various instruments interact. Now listen again to the song as a whole.

Note

Even if a high can enhance the selective focus of your attention on certain perceptions, sensations and memories or other thought processes; this does not mean that we can sustain this selective focus for long. On the contrary: the high of some, less favorable varieties can make us become more "jumpy" in your attention. We focus on the taste of chocolate, then we quickly associatively jump to a strong focus on a memory of our last birthday, then jump to focus on the music playing in the background, and so forth, in rapid succession.

I call this "jumpy hyperfocus". You may be hyperfocused for a short period of time on various perceptions, thoughts and memories or bodily sensations, but you are jumping often in your attention. Complex thought processes can become difficult.

If you want to use the hyperfocus of attention during a
high without being too jumpy then use fresh cannabis
in a vaporizer, try using a lower dosage if necessary and
choose your environment carefully: make sure you do
not have too many distracting things around you while
you are high.

In general, the repeated practice of meditation can help
you hold your attention longer – not just during a high.

Experiment

Enter the "Here-and-Now"

You can use this focus of attention to come to a better appreciation of the here-and-now of existence, as many cannabis users have reported.

During a high, take a shower and concentrate on your body. Can you feel where your tensions are? Do you feel how your body parts relax? Stay in the here-and-now of experience, focus on perceiving the effects of the water on your body.

The Enjoyment of Taste

Many cannabis varieties can enhance your appetite and your experience of taste. If we learn how to use the high, our taste experience gets intensified, and we can learn how to explore sensual nuances in taste experiences. We should, therefore, not waste our appetite on mindlessly consuming cheap sweets or fast food.

If you use your high to set out to explore complex natural tastes then you can discover or re-discover the value of many foods and change their meaning to you forever.

Experiment

A Universe in a Hazelnut

When you are high, eat some natural organic food of a high quality – a fresh, local strawberry; roasted hazelnuts from the Piedmont region of Italy; Medjool dates from Morocco or whatever exquisite food you like to explore.

Make your experience unforgettable. Try to discriminate between the various aspects in what you taste
and describe your taste experience.

Travelling to the Past

Countless cannabis users have reported that they can remember episodes from their past better during a high. Many remember long gone events even from their early childhood in vivid details, as if they were re-living them all over again.

Experiment

A Trip to Your Trip

Create a playlist of songs you associate with a specific period in your life. Inhale three or four times from a vaporizer, then wait for 10 to 15 minutes until you have reached a pleasant high. Inhale more if necessary. Listen to the music and look at some old photos from that time to help you remember. Choose a memorable event like a trip to Vietnam. Get comfortable and then close your eyes. Do you remember events or details of events that you usually would not remember when thinking about this period of time? Maybe even events in your childhood? Try to remember not only external events, but also your past feelings; your thoughts; moods and your former self. How did you feel in those situations? Take short notes of memories, if
they feel valuable to you.

One of the best methods to travel into your own past and to re-live your memories is a good massage during a high in which you relax and focus on remembering. This can also be a great setting for a first high, as long as you feel comfortable with the person giving you a massage.

The Power of Imagination

Many cannabis users have reported that a high can enhance their imagination - not only their ability to invoke images but also to imagine new melodies or sounds when composing a song. Or even to imagine the complex taste of a new dessert creation made of dark chocolate, mango purée and coconut yoghurt.

Obviously, an enhanced imagination can be used for many creative activities.

The Running Elephant

This is an experiment for a medium to strong high. During your high, relax for a while and close your eyes. Music can help you to freely associate thoughts. Now try to imagine a running elephant. Keep the image as long as possible in your imagination.

How does your elephant look? What color is it? How big is it? How does it move? Does it look real, or more like a cartoon elephant? Are the images changing in your mind? Can you see a little movie where your elephant comes to life? What does it do?

A Special Animated Movie

When I was in my early 20s, I watched an animated short movie of an acquaintance of mine at a movie festival. The movie was drawn by hand and artistically outstanding in its style. It was also different from other animated shorts in one important aspect: while others leave the image of a background landscape more or less static and only create new frames for the moving figures and parts, every frame in this movie had been completely re-drawn. As a result, the landscapes, the trees, the houses, everything in the movie seemed to move and jiggle a little.

Everything seemed to be alive.

Years later during a strong high I closed my eyes and imagined an animated movie scene in the very same style. I was stunned, then, because it was clear to me that I did not just remember the movie I had seen but that my imagination had re-created a scene in the visual style of this movie, but with different content. I had started my imagination trying to visualize a certain scenery but then the images started to flow from my mind without conscious control.

While high, my mind created new animated imagery of a bird cage, the door of the cage opened and the birds flew away into a beautiful landscape and I followed them as if I was flying behind them, until the flock of birds morphed into a different scenery. I followed this visual 'trip' like an internal movie. It was breathtaking.

Imagination and Decision Making

Neuroscientists like Michael Gazzaniga remind us that imagination is not only useful for creative purposes. We need it in everyday life to make important decisions. If I get a job offer and come back from my first job interview, I will probably imagine how it would be to work for that company. How would it be to interact on a daily basis with the people I have met? To sit in that office and work in that room, looking down at the streets of Barcelona five times a week?

An enhanced ability for imagination during a high can therefore help us to make important decisions in our lives.

We can also use this enhanced ability for imagination, for instance to follow a guided meditation where we are asked to imagine certain sceneries.

Mind Racing

According to reports of users and my own experience, some varieties of cannabis seem to lead to mind racing, while others tend to have a more calming and focusing effect. Many users find it difficult to "ride the wave". They feel like they are chasing trains of thought they can't follow anymore at such a fast speed.

We need to learn how different varieties have an effect on us concerning the aspect of mind racing. It can certainly also be influenced by dosage. A racing mind can be helpful in a creative phase where you have to spin out many ideas, but it can also be counterproductive when you have to actually sit down and get into the process of writing or working further on the idea you already had.

Experiment

Let Your Mind Race

During a stronger high, lay down, close your eyes, and freely associate – alone or with friends. For instance, think of a word like "palm tree" or "friendship" and let your mind race to all the memories or associations that come up. You may end up with interesting distant memories or other associations.

Use this method to freely associate in connection with a subject of interest to you. Think of a friend; a situation; a theoretical concept; a creative project or a theory.

You will need to gain experience with different cannabis varieties and dosages to control mindracing during a high. A racing mind can be helpful in a creative phase where you need to generate a lot of ideas, but it can also be counterproductive if you want to work out a particular idea without constantly digressing, for example.

Finding New Patterns

During a high we often discover new patterns or find similarities between different patterns we have perceived in the past. Pattern recognition is essential in our lives. We can perceive and discriminate a pattern in the way someone is flirting with us or we can recognize the pride of a young child in the way they are riding their bike. There is a characteristic visual pattern in a sarcastic smile of a friend, a distinctive pattern in the nervous sound of a fearful a voice or in the subdued tense behavior of a predator in the wild, a panther for example, right before it is about to attack. Patterns are everywhere. Sometimes, your observations of patterns during a high may seem trivial, but they can also lead to deep, life-changing insights. It is important that you take notes if you feel you have made an interesting observation during a high. If you read your notes later, you will often remember more details of your perception during a high than those you write down. You can then evaluate your observation all over again.

Experiment

Hunting for Patterns

Think about interesting patterns in your area of expertise. Maybe you are a musician, a painter or do you like movies?

During a high, take notes of the patterns you see in a painting style from a certain painter. Can you see similarities to other painters? Can you recognize other influences?

As a musician, can you do the same for patterns in the playing style of a certain musician?

When you watch a movie, think about the storyline or the plot. Is its pattern similar to other movies you have seen?

Mood Modulation

A cannabis high can have interesting mood modulating effects by directly affecting neuromodulatory mechanisms. The effects of THC are predominantly described as euphoric, anti-depressive and anxiolytic (reducing fear). However, the change in mood during a high depends on various factors such as other compounds of a certain cannabis variety that modulate the high, set and setting and dose. As we have seen, higher doses of THC may as well lead also to temporary anxiety and paranoia.

The mood modulation effects of cannabis can be importantly different depending on the variety we use. So, depending on their chemical profile, there are cannabis varieties better known for a happy, euphoric effect, while others can also have a rather negative or depressing effect on the mood.

As a user, you should mindfully observe how certain varieties affect your mood in order to select a variety that best suits your individual purposes and needs.

Most medical scientific perspectives on cannabis and mood modulation ignore how the multi-dimensional cognitive effects of a cannabis high affect mood modulation. For example, a high can bring back long-forgotten memories of childhood, which can bring a lot of happiness. However, if a high brings back long-forgotten traumatic memories, it can also temporarily lead to very negative and painful emotions.

Recognizing new patterns during a high can also lead to changes in our mood. If we suddenly realize during a high that we keep reacting to the criticism of a beloved friend with the same wrong behavior pattern, for example, this can make us feel sad – but we can also feel relieved and deeply content, if we feel that we can now take a personal development step with it.

Interestingly, substances like THC or limonene with a direct effect on our neuromodular chemistry can facilitate cognitive enhancements during a high. For example, a anxiety-relieving effect may facilitate introspective insights on a topic such as our own mortality, a subject which we may usually be too afraid or unwilling to think about.

In short, then, mood modulation during a high is a complex story – dependent on dose, variety, set and setting - and we have to take into account that our moods are interdependent with various cognitive effects.

Generally, though, varieties of cannabis high in THC – if not used to excess – will tend to bring euphoric and antidepressant effects.

The Slowdown of Time

During a high time often seems to pass very slowly, the experience of the taste of chocolate ice cream can seem to be endless. This slowdown in our perception of time may be caused by some other cognitive effects which cannabis can have on our mind. While high, our mind often races, and we make big associative leaps in our thinking.

We are hyperfocusing on some activity, while remembering certain events, watching a movie or imagining certain situations.

We observe a dog playing with a ball in the park for two minutes, and while we are doing this, we hyperfocus on our associations, maybe on memories, remembering dozens of scenes with our own dog and other freely associated situations.

When we then bring back our attention to our environment and check the clock, we notice that only two minutes have passed, but we feel as if we had gone through a long journey in our mind that would usually take half an hour.

The slowdown in our time perception brings certain dangers, while driving for instance, because we can lose our temporal orientation.

Yet, in a safe environment, you can use this slowdown in the perception of time to subjectively prolong the experience of a splash in the pool on a hot summer's day, which then feels like eternal bliss.

Slowing Down Time

Relax, get high (medium to intense) and start a playlist of songs. Close your eyes and let your thoughts run free. Do not try to keep track of time. Just listen and let your mind wander. After a while, take a look at your playlist and check how much time has passed since you started listening. How long did you actually listen to the music? How long did it feel to you?

A New Experience of Our Body

Many cannabis varieties generate a high leading to an intensified perception of our own bodily sensations.

We then often attend more to our bodies and can feel more intensely and in more detail the feeling of a sip of cold water running down our throat; discover the stiffness in our neck from a long day of work at the computer or we immensely enjoy the warmth of the sun on our skin. A cannabis high can bring us back into our bodies.

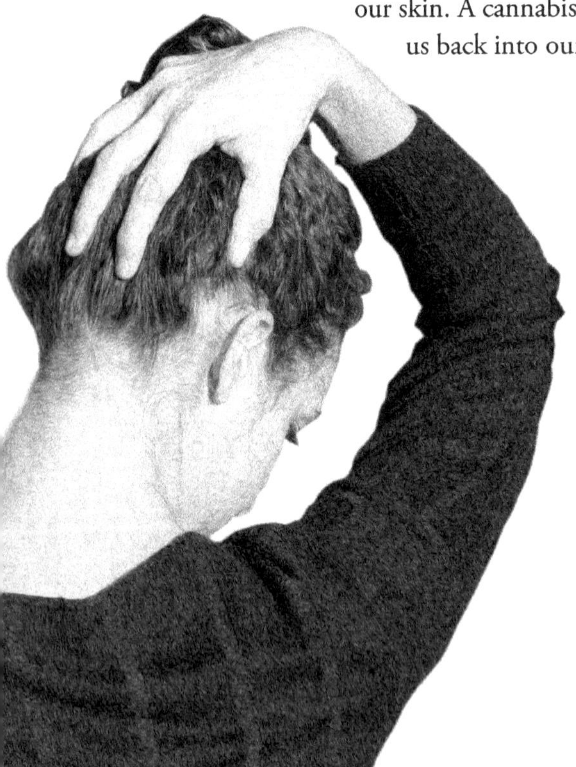

Experiment

Travelling Into Your Body

If you are already experienced and feel comfortable getting high, choose a variety you know that has a stronger effect on your body perception and take a warm bath during a high. Or if possible, visit hot springs or a natural mineral bath. Make sure that you are safe and functional at all times.

Close your eyes. Direct your attention to your toes, your feet, your legs and then upwards through your body. Feel how the warm water relaxes your body and soothes your tenseness. Become aware of the intensity and the acuity of your bodily perceptions.

Can you now discover tense spots in your body that you weren't aware of before? Think about what you can do to avoid such tensions in the future.

Story

An Insight During A Yoga Session

Some years ago I decided to get high to do some yoga exercises during which I would bend forward to touch my feet. Now, although my other yoga abilities are decent, my forward bend always looks a bit silly. I can't bend down as far as I want, which is probably the result of years of practicing various sports without enough stretching. I am ambitious when it comes to sports, so I always tried to get deeper than I actually should during these yoga exercises.

This time, when I did the exercise high I felt the intense pain of stretching too far and became aware of the fact that my ambition and my vanity were leading me to go too deep into the stretch. I felt how my breathing became shallow and how my muscles became tenser. "I am alone here", I thought, "Who do I want to impress?"

So, I relaxed, forced myself to relax, but kept trying with less force, just to the point where it felt right.

After a few seconds, my breathing became deeper.
I relaxed, mentally, but also physically. My muscles
and my tendons became more supple. Without trying harder, I suddenly got deeper and deeper and then
stayed at a point where it still felt right. I could still
breathe deeply. And I had never come that far in this
position before.

I will always remember this enhanced bodily feeling and
this insight. It may not have changed world politics and
I could have learned it easily enough from a decent yoga
teacher, but it changed my yoga forever.

I also learned a lesson for life. Our efforts will often be
rewarded, and intensifying the effort will usually lead to
more success; but if we force something as much as we
can for the wrong reasons, it will not get us as far as a
mindfully reflected effort.

Through Your Body Into Your Mind

Many of your bodily sensations represent psychological states, moods, memories or attitudes. While high, mindfully travel with your attention through your body. Where do you feel tense, sore or stressed? Where do you feel you more relaxed, energized?

The intensification of your bodily sensations during a high helps you to focus and to discover more about yourself. Maybe you can see some new patterns now.

Can you feel how the mental stress from your work caused stiffness in your shoulders and neck? Or maybe you feel a wonderful, relaxed looseness in your muscles after making an important decision or meeting a deadline?

Find out how much your bodily sensations can tell you about your psyche.

The Inner Voyage

A high can help us to come to introspective insights in many ways – if we are ready for it. We travel into our past and vividly remember past perspectives on the world.

We can remember many situations bearing a certain similarity. For instance, we can ask ourselves in which past situations we acted courageously. We will then often freely associate in rapid succession many other situations from our childhood and adolescence or even more recently in which we also acted courageously. This can help us to see patterns in our past behavior, which in turn can help us to understand whether we really are courageous or not.

A cannabis high can therefore help us to discover our weaknesses and strengths, our character and dispositions. And we can use these introspective insights to grow on a personal level.

During a high, we can then associate many such past situations in rapid succession from our memory in which we acted bravely or cowardly. This can help us identify patterns of behavior in our lives and understand whether or not we are truly courageous.

In other words, a high can help us discover our weaknesses and strengths, our character and our dispositions. And these introspective insights can then help us begin personal development.

"Failure to read what is happening in another's soul is not easily seen as a cause of unhappiness: but those who fail to attend the motions of their own soul are necessarily unhappy."

Marc Aurelius, Philosopher and Roman Emperor

Experiment

A Question of Courage

While high, get comfortable in a place where you can concentrate on yourself. Close your eyes and ask yourself in which situations you have acted courageously in your life. Try to remember situations in your life where you had to make important decisions, or in which you had to show courage. Can you remember these situations and how you felt in them? Did you hesitate? Did you feel anxious?

How have you changed? Are you more courageous now than you were as a child or a teenager?

Take short notes about your personal insights.

Empathic Understanding

Many cannabis users have reported they find it easier to simulate the perspective of others during a high. They feel they are able to better understand how others feel and think, and report wonderful insights into their character, their moods and dispositions. They suddenly recognize behavioral patterns in others of which they were completely unaware before.

Cannabis and Autism

In recent years we have seen that some highly autistic children can benefit immensely from medical cannabis. During a high, they are suddenly able to make more eye contact; they smile at their parents and start to play with them instead of acting aggressively. They laugh and imitate behavior in a way that they had not been able to do previously.

The ability to empathically understand others and to see themselves in their situation seems to strongly improve in many cases. Here we can clearly see how valuable the psychoactive effects of cannabis can be even for severe medical disorders.

Experiment

The Voyage Into Another Self

During a high of medium strength, think of somebody who is in a situation that you don't know well. For instance, take a look at a photo of somebody standing on a huge cliff about to jump into the ocean. Can you see things from their perspective? How does it feel?

Then, think about your last argument with a friend or partner. Can you put yourself in their shoes to understand how they perceived the situation and how they felt?

Take short notes about your observations.

Enhancing Creativity

We know that a long list of artists, musicians, writers and comedians have used cannabis to enhance their creative work. During a high many of the cognitive effects I have mentioned before can help creative processes in various ways. The hyperfocus of attention; an enhancement of imagination; an enhanced pattern recognition or the heightened ability to empathically understand others can all help to achieve interesting creative results in your work.

But we have to learn how to use a high – without experience and know-how, a high can also negatively affect
our creative output. For instance, a subjective change
in the perception of time can interfere with a musician's
timing. There is a whole spectrum of creative activities
which all demand different cognitive and motor skills. A
creative jazz trumpet solo on stage needs perfect hand-
eye control, timing and a rapid flow of spontaneous
ideas concerning musical variations. When you
write a poem, you are in a completely different process. Hand-eye coordination
and sense of time do not matter so
much.

If we want to benefit creatively from a high we have to learn how cannabis can help us with certain creative activities. A high affects a whole spectrum of cognitive processes, and various creative activities depend on different sets of cognitive abilities. We therefore have to learn about the right dosage, the cannabis variety and many other factors influencing our performance. We also have to learn in which phase of a certain creative activity a high can help or hinder us.

Take for example the creative activity of writing a novel.
Some writers can concentrate really well during a high
and are more able to get into the
flow of writing.

Psychologist Mihály Csikszentmihályi describes the
mental state of „flow“ as one in which we are completely
focused and oblivious to an activity, working or thinking
at the peak of our performance; time flies and nothing
else matters. For Csikszentmihályi, this is a state that
makes us deeply happy.

Others, however, may experience that they are able to
generate outstanding ideas during a high, but come
to the understanding that a high interferes with their
flow during the writing phase, because of what I called
"jumpy hyperfocus". They'd rather take short notes
while high and then start writing at a later time when
they are straight.

So those who want to use cannabis to enhance their creativity need to experiment for themselves and find out for what kind of creative endeavor and at what stage of the process a high can best help – and whether it can help at all.

Shawn Gold, founder and CEO of *Pilgrim Soul* (pilgrimsoul.com), offers a Creative Thinking Journal which he recommends to be used while we are high. It is an excellent tool to learn more about using cannabis for creative purposes.

Phases of Creativity

Choose a creative activity you like – sketching; painting; photography; composing or playing music; graphic design or writing a short story – whatever you like. While you are high try to use your altered state of mind in various phases of this activity. Find out which phase the high can help you and in which, if any, it interferes negatively with your creative output.

For instance, if you want to write a short story, maybe the high helps you to think of ideas for the story, or maybe just the characters? Does it also help you to actually sit down, concentrate and write the whole story? Or maybe it helps in a last phase when you have already written a draft and you then go on and edit the content of your story?

Maybe being high enhances your landscape photography insofar as it helps you to perceive unusual moods? Or maybe it helps in a final, later phase when you're in post-processing and experimenting with different effects and filters? Then again, a high may negatively affect your ability to operate you camera equipment correctly?

Find out which intensity of a high you need and which varieties you find most helpful. Maybe an intense, dreamy high helps you to visualize great ideas but a light buzz helps you more in the editing phase?

Take notes.

Funny Stuff

In the 1920s, German philosopher and essayist Walter Benjamin experimented with large doses of cannabis to come to profound insights, and he succeeded, as I argue in my book "What Hashish Did To Walter Benjamin". He did have great insights – and he also came up with funny stuff. During one session after ingesting a large dosage of hashish, Benjamin wrote in his high protocol:

"If Freud would psychoanalyze God's creation, the Fjords wouldn't come off very well."

Clearly, cannabis can help us to understand the subtleties in a funny or absurd situation better, to get an unusual perspective on details of patterns in the world. During a high, for example, we may suddenly understand that our colleague subconsciously imitates the accent of Al Pacino in

Music

A cannabis high can change our perception and cognition in many ways and, thus enhance our ability to perceive, understand, and produce music.

It can lead to an enhanced ability to focus and to come into the flow of rapid creative improvisation or to see and invent new patterns. It also changes our perception of time, an influence that clearly reflects in the rhythm and flow of musical traditions heavily influenced by the use of cannabis, such as jazz music.

A high can enhance our ability to understand others better, which helps a band to get into a groove while playing together.

Cannabis use has deeply affected the course of our music history and had a profound impact on recent music genres like jazz; reggae; rock; pop; hip hop; trip hop and electronic music.

It has affected musical traditions for hundreds or thousands or maybe even tens of thousands of years, such as in African music where cannabis leaves and flowers were thrown onto bonfires for nocturnal healing rites that included dancing, singing and drumming.

Insights

During a high we often relax and our mind wanders.
We associate freely and see new patterns, or we may
find similarities in patterns and come up with new ideas
seemingly out of nowhere.

Many cannabis users have reported that they have gener-
ated deep, spontaneous insights during a high. I have
extensively argued in my previous work that this is not
a myth; some insights during a high may actually turn
out to be nonsense or funny, but others can be really
fascinating, profound and valuable.

Value your high for giving you these gifts. You may find
some gems. Or, at the very least, have something to
laugh about.

Again, most importantly, take a short note if you believe you have a meaningful insight during a high. You usually do not have to note down all the details – you will remember them later. Leave a notepad or something else beside your bed or on your couch or wherever you often get high so that you will have something close.

Later, take a look at your notes and try to evaluate whether there is a gem that may turn into something bigger. This could be a personal insight into your character; an idea for a book title; a new business opportunity; an idea about a conversation you need to have with your partner or a series of photos you may want to start taking.

Living with Cannabis

Riding a High Like a Wave

The cannabis high can enhance many types of activities. Yet we have to learn how to ride a high – like a surfer has to learn how to use his surfboard to ride an ocean wave. The surfer needs to acquire knowledge and skills to balance on a board while standing up on it in the water.

If we do not learn these skills, then cannabis can have a serious negative impact on our lives and the lives of those around us.

Cannabis, Meditation and Culture

For centuries cannabis has been used for meditation and inspirational purposes – amongst others by Indian sadhus, ascetics practicing yoga to achieve liberation through meditation and the contemplation of God, Tantric traditions like Vamacara and Tantra of the left hand path as well as other groups within Buddhism, Sufism and the Rastafarians.

A cannabis high can help us to focus, to meditate and to come and stay in the here-and-now of the moment.

Many cannabis users have reported that the experience of the high encouraged them to explore and try out new meditation practices. Practicing meditation can also help us to sustain our focus during a high and to get into a "flow" state of mind during a creative or meaningful activity.

Experiment

Meditation and Imagination

Listen to a guided meditation that entertains visualizations in which you are asked to imagine various situations. A good source would be Jack Kornfield's ‚Guided Meditations for Beginners'.

At first, do the meditation without being high. Then, try the mediation during a medium to strong high. Did your concentration change? Is the visualization now more intense? Can you find a difference in your ability to relive certain events and to produce various associations?

The Zen Buddhist Thích Nhất Hanh inspired me to
do a walking meditation that I can highly recommend.
While walking through nature, give yourself five to ten
minutes of saying aloud or silently in your mind the
word "come" when you take a step left and the word
"to" when you take a right step. You walk and always
arrive back in the here-and-now. Keep your eyes open
and gaze, just to navigate. Again, try this high or sober.

Include this routine into your life.

Meditation – High or Sober?

One of the most fundamental effects of the
cannabis high is to focus our attention which may also
help us to be present, to come to the "here-and -now" of
existence. Obviously, this can help beginners in particular with their practice of meditation.

But does a high really help us to get "deeper" in the meditation? Or does the high hinder you in getting into a "pure" state of meditative contemplation? Does being high really help to experience the higher realms of consciousness of which so many traditions speak?

There are different opinions on this, often differing within each tradition.

A Multitude of Altered States of Consciousness

There are many techniques of meditation, and they do not all serve the same purpose. You may want to meditate to achieve a better mental focus in your everyday life, or you may use guided meditation of a different kind to explore and heal a traumatic experience. There is no one state of meditation, neither is there one "high". As we have seen, many factors determine what kind of high you can experience.

Combining a high with a meditation technique certainly enriches the realm of possible altered states of consciousness that you can experience to lead a richer and more fulfilled life. Whether you want to use this combination and for how long and for what purpose certainly depends heavily on individual needs.

Love, Sex and the Cannabis High

Throughout history, a cannabis high has been used by millions of people to enhance their sexual encounters. It plays a big role in the Indian mythology and was also used by the cannabis-loving god Shiva, who is also symbolized by a penis ("lingam"), and often portrayed as standing in a vagina ("yoni").

In some lines of the Yogic and Tantric tradition the cannabis high was used to produce a state of sexual ecstasy which is also supposed to bring about a state of enlightenment.

A high can enhance your love life in many wonderful ways. But it can also bring problems.

Some cannabis users have reported that a high makes them tired, confused or too introspective and self-involved for sexual encounters. If we want to use a high positively for sex we have to make sure that we get some things right first:

- Make sure that all participants are experienced or at least feel fine with you using cannabis

- If somebody is inexperienced with a high or if one of you feels overwhelmed by a high it can interfere negatively with your lovemaking

- If all participants involved in a sexual encounter are high, it is easier to find a common level of communication

- The choice of your variety of cannabis can make a big difference. Some varieties are more sexually arousing; some may lead to vaginal dryness and some may make you too tired. Experiment. Try to get your cannabis fresh and well cured

- Start with a low dosage and then experiment with your partner how far you can go as to the intensity of your high.

- Make sure that you are in a safe and comfortable environment.

Many users tend to underestimate the positive potential of cannabis for lovemaking. As we have seen, cannabis can enhance many cognitive processes and have interesting mood-altering effects which can positively influence our sexual experiences:

- Some varieties can have a strong aphrodisiac effect on us

- Hyperfocusing on our bodily sensations can strongly take us into the here-and-now, relax us and let us forget about our daily stress and routines.

- The concentration on the here-and-now and possible additional anxiolytic effects of some cannabis varieties help us to lose our inhibitions which can be especially important in the taboo-inflicted sexual realm.

- Bodily sensations like stroking, kissing and penetration are felt with much more intensity and acuity. We delve into the richness of experience.

- Time seems to flow in slow motion; pleasurable experiences like an orgasm feel much longer than usual. and feel what they really yearn for.

- It is easier for us to find patterns in our behavior, which facilitates non-verbal communication and leads to a closer intimacy.

- We can empathically understand our partner better and feel what they really yearn for.

- Our enhanced pattern recognition abilities during a high can help us to identify long-standing routines and to transcend them.

- Our imagination becomes intensified and imagination can definitely play a central role during sex.

- We become more creative and eager to try out new things. Creativity is one of the most important components of a fulfilled sex life.

- Some women who vaginally applied cannabis extracts have reported that they feel less pain during penetration and have fewer problems with cramping

As with creativity, the temporary effects of a cannabis high can lead to wonderful enhancements of your love life but it can also negatively interfere with your ability to respond to your partner in many ways. Some users have felt they become too introspective or too anxious when high. Again, users need to learn and acquire various skills as they mindfully explore this field.

Experiment

The Infinity of Sensuality

Use your altered sense of time during a high to slow things down during a sexual encounter. Take your time. Observe the body language of your partner and let his or her lust guide you. Follow your curiosity and your intensified imagination.

Don't take notes.

Cannabis and Relationships

Cannabis is not only a mighty aphrodisiac that can magnificently enhance sexual encounters. If we use a high mindfully and with experience, we can enhance the communication in our relationship and start to be more perceptive and creative in dealing with our partners.

Many users have reported that their use of cannabis has led to a better introspective understanding of their behavior, to a deeper empathic understanding of their partners and to greater intimacy as well as to healing processes in their relationships. For wonderful personal stories during a high take a look at my friend Lester Grinspoon's magnificent website project, *marijuana-uses. com.*

Escapism and Personal Development

Heavy long-term cannabis consumption can have a very negative impact on some user's love lives and their relationships – and for some, on their social life in general. A large proportion of cannabis users today probably get high mostly to escape from their mundane day-to-day troubles into the bliss of the here-and-now. We all need those little escapes sometimes. But many are abusing the high to escape too often and to stop accepting the challenges of modern life.

It is up to us whether we use cannabis positively to start a voyage or to gain introspective or empathic insights and to grow personally, or to abuse it for chronic escapism.

Cannabis and Addiction

Compared to legal substances like alcohol and tobacco, cannabis is hardly physically addictive. Make no mistake, some users have undergone severe withdrawal symptoms after they quit using cannabis such as severe headaches sweating, sleeping problems and bad mood swings. These withdrawal symptoms, however, usually vanish within a few days or weeks.

But cannabis can also be a factor in leading to a psychological addiction which can have a severe negative impact on our lives. How can we find out if our use has become an unhealthy addiction? Can daily use of cannabis be problematic?

Regular or even daily use of cannabis does not necessarily constitute an addiction nor should it be termed as abuse.

We always have to ask ourselves:

Is my use of cannabis still good for me? Does it enhance my life or does it stop me from accepting important challenges? Has my cannabis use become a habit that is rather damaging to me and those close to me? Or does it still help me to lead a more meaningful life?

If they are unprejudiced and open-minded, your loved ones, friends and relatives will help you to answer these questions. If you feel like they cannot help you seek a professional therapist you trust in that matter.

Tolerance

If we use cannabis several times a week or on a daily basis we can develop a tolerance to it, meaning that we need higher dosages to get an effect. Why? Our endo-cannabinoid may show an intelligent reaction. One interesting scientific hypothesis about the development of tolerance states that when the ECS is constantly flooded with consumed phytocannabinoids, this results in a constantly over-stimulated fine-tuned signaling system which then intelligently responds by downregu-lating endocannabinoid receptors to stay in balance.

In a way, this effect can be positively used, for instance by patients who need to use large amounts of cannabis over a long period to treat their chronic pain. They can use large amounts of psychoactive cannabis to treat their pains without getting too high – and many of them only want to get pain relief without being high all the time.

But if you want to use the cannabis high to experience
the cognitive enhancements described in this book, then
you should be careful not to develop a strong tolerance
because you may not benefit from many of the psychoactive effects even at large dosages. The good news is
that if you take a tolerance break, your endocannabinoid
receptors will be back to normal after just a few days
or up to four weeks depending on how much and how
frequently you used cannabis.

For some users taking a tolerance break or getting off
frequent and long-term cannabis can lead to some
withdrawal symptoms like sleeplessness and moodiness.
These symptoms are rather mild compared to withdrawal from alcohol or other substances but they should
not be underestimated.

The Journey of Life

"But the true voyagers are only those who leave
Just to be leaving; hearts light, like balloons,
They never turn aside from their fatality
And without knowing why they always say: ‚Let's go!'"

Les Fleurs du Mal, Le Voyage by Charles Baudelaire

Life is a journey, a journey to the inner realms of
ourselves but also into the world of nature; art; music;
culture; technology; the cosmos and into the thousands
of fascinating minds of others: friends and family; artists
and writers; filmmakers; thinkers; travelers and many
other beings. The cannabis high is one of many altered
states of consciousness, through which we can travel –
further into the realm of our own present experience,
into our character and past and into the reality and endless subtleties of other selves.

It can help us to generate insights about the world
around us. We can use it to elevate our mood, to relax
or occasionally take a rest from our daily chores and
sorrows or to work creatively; to more easily make better
decisions and to personally grow.

Cannabis, like other psychoactive substances, can be a
companion and a means of transportation on our life's
journey helping us to travel to new locations and to
understand the patterns we live in.

Some of us may decide to avoid the risks and problems
associated with cannabis use. Others will choose to
use it for some time in their lives or even to use it as a
lifetime companion. We all have to decide for ourselves
if, how and for how long we want to use the potential of
this unique mind-altering plant.

In principle, there is nothing wrong with altered states of consciousness. Some are pathological and should be treated accordingly but many altered states are an important part of our nature. Altered states that we induce ourselves such as meditation; ecstatic dance; trance, LSD trips; hypnosis or the cannabis high hold great potential in addition to risks. If we want to benefit from them, we must master the art of finding a balance between these states and embedding each of them meaningfully in our lives.

Sleep for instance is necessary and wonderful but too much or not enough of it can ruin your existence. Ecstasy is an altered state of consciousness we seek but we cannot have it all the time – and living without it is not necessarily desirable, either.

It is in our nature to experience different states of consciousness and also to seek further states in order to enhance our consciousness. This points us to an important political dimension:

We will have to stand up for the basic right of cognitive liberty, the freedom to control our own consciousness. We need to be allowed to freely alter our consciousness as long as we do not harm others by doing so. Also we should demand that we are allowed to decide for ourselves whether and how others shall be allowed to alter our consciousness with drugs or by other mind-altering means.

For more information on this general subject matter please visit the *Center for Cognitive Liberty & Ethics* at *www.cognitiveliberty.org*.

The cannabis high allows us to have temporary transformations of consciousness that can contribute to our personal balance and enrich our lives. It is up to us to claim this potential and to learn the art of using it skillfully.

"We are shaped by our thoughts; we become what we think. When the mind is pure, joy follows like a shadow that never leaves."

Buddha

My Deepest Gratitude

Thanks to Thích Nhat Hanh and his wonderful book How to Sit, which inspired the style and structure of this book.

I would like to express my wholehearted thanks to my friend Michael Zöllner for his many valuable suggestions and for being such a generous help over so many years.

My good friend and mentor Lester Grinspoon has seen earlier versions of this book and was delighted to see it come into existence. I am immensely grateful to him for the many years of friendship and collaboration, and his willingness to share and discuss his incredible knowledge with me. Sadly, he could not live to see the publication of this book.

Big thanks also to Pierre Debs for sharing his insights into the endocannabinoid system and for his incredible support over the years.

Thanks so much, Carlos Schtang, for reading and editing this book in English.

Peter Leis and Dylan Lord, thank you for your helpful feedback on the manuscript.

My friends Gregory Frye and Joe Dolce, thanks for your ongoing support and valuable feedback!

My deep gratitude also goes to my father who wanted to help me illustrate this book. Unfortunately his progressive illness made this impossible.

Many thanks also to my wife Nadja for proofreading the German version and your patience, which was almost as great as that of our daughter Jella, who so often sat on my lap and watched me work on title versions or layouts of the book.

In the end, it helped a lot to be occasionally pulled by the ears by an impatient little girl and reminded that the book needed to be finished and that life goes on.

Suggested Literature and Links

The Endocannabinoid System (ECS)

Clarke, T.L.; Johnson, R.L.; Simone, J.J.; Carlone, R.L. (2021) The Endocannabinoid System and Invertebrate Neurodevelopment and Regeneration. Int. J. Mol. Sci.,22,2103. https://doi.org/10.3390/ijms22042103

Di Marzo, Vincenzo and Piscitelli, Fabiana (2015) The Endocannabinoid System and its Modulation by Phytocannabinoids. Neurotherapeutics. 12(4): 692–698. https://pubmed.ncbi.nlm.nih.gov/26271952/

Kruk-Slomka M, Dzik A, Budzynska B, Biala G. (2017) Endocannabinoid System: the Direct and Indirect Involvement in the Memory and Learning Processes – a Short Review. Mol Neurobiol.;54(10):8332-8347. Doi:10.1007/s12035-016-0313-5

Mechoulam, Raphael (2007). The Endocannabinoids: Functional Roles and Therapeutic Opportunities. European Neuropsychopharmacology 17. Doi: 10.1016/S0924-977X(07)70165-7.

Piscitelli, F., Di Marzo, V. (2021) Cannabinoids: a class of unique natural products with unique pharmacology. Rend. Fis. Acc. Lincei 32, 5–15 https://doi.org/10.1007/s12210-020-00966-y

Plant Intelligence

Wohleben, Peter, Billinghurst, Jane, et al. (2016) The Hidden Life of Trees: What They Feel, How They Communicate-Discoveries from A Secret World. Greystone Books; First English Language Edition, 8th Printing (13. September 2016)

Animals and Psychoactive Substances

Siegel, Ronald K. (1989) Intoxication. The Universal Drive for Mind-Altering Substances, Park Street Press, Vermont

Cannabis-Evolution, Culture, and Prohibition

Abel, Ernest L. (1982), Marijuana. The First Twelve Thousand Years. McGraw-Hill paperback edition, New York.

The Emperor Wears No Clothes: A History of Cannabis/ Hemp/Marijuana), Independently published, 1985

Lee, Martin A. (2012) Smoke Signals: A Social History of Marijuana – Medical, Recreational and Scientific, Scribner.

McPartland, J. M., Guy, G. W. (2004). "The evolution of cannabis and coevolution with the cannabinoid receptor – a hypothesis," in The medicinal uses of cannabis and cannabinoids. Eds. Guy, G. W., Whittle, B. A., Robson, P. J. (London: Pharmaceutical Press), 71–101.

Pollan, Michael (2002) The Botany of Desire: A Plant's-Eye View of the World. Random House Trade Paper Backs.

Phyto-Cannabinoids, The Indica-Sativa Debate, Entourage Effects

Abioye A, Ayodele O, Marinkovic A, Patidar R, Akinwekomi A, Sanyaolu A. (2020) Δ9-Tetrahydrocannabivarin (THCV): a commentary on potential therapeutic benefit for the management of obesity and diabetes. J Cannabis Res. Jan 31;2(1):6. doi: 10.1186/s42238-020-0016-7.

Clarke RC, Merlin MD. (2013) Cannabis Evolution and Ethnobotany. University of California Press, Berkeley

Clarke, RC, Merlin, MD. (2016) Cannabistaxonomy: The 'sativa' vs. 'indica' debate. HerbalGram 110: 44–49.

EISohly, M. (2002) Chemical Constituents of Cannabis. In: Cannabis and Cannabinoids — Pharmacology, Toxicology, and Therapeutic Potential. The Haworth Press; S. 27-36.

Hazekamp,et al.; Cannabis: From Cultivar to Chemovar II—A Metabolomics Approach to Cannabis Classification. Cannabis and Cannabinoid Research 2016,1.1 http://online.liebertpub.com/doi/10.1089/can.2016.0017

Jiang, Caifu, Mithani, Aziz, Xiangchao Gan, Belfield, Eric J. , Klingler, John P., Zhu, Jian-Kang, Ragoussis, Jiannis, Mott, Richard,. Harberd. Nicholas P (2011) Regenerant Arabidopsis Lineages Display a Distinct Genome-Wide Spectrum of Mutations Conferring Variant Phenotypes. Current Biology, 2011; doi: 10.1016/j.cub.2011.07.002

McPartland, J. M., and Guy, G. W. (2017) Models of cannabis taxonomy, cultural bias, and conflicts between scientific and vernacular names. Bot. Rev. 83, 327–381. doi: 10.1007/s12229-017-9187-0

McPartland, J. M. (2018) Cannabis systematics at the levels of family, genus and species. Cannabis & Cannabinoid Res. 3, 203–212. doi: 10.1089/can.2018.0039

Niesink, RJ, van Laar MW. (2013) Does Cannabidiol Protect Against Adverse Psychological Effects of THC? Front Psychiatry. 2013;4:130. Oct 16. doi:10.3389/fpsyt.2013.00130

Russo, Ethan Budd (2011) Taming THC: potential cannabis synergy and phytocannabinoid-terpenoid entourage effects. British Journal of Pharmacology 1631344–1364

CBD

Hudson, R., Renard, J., Norris, C., Rushlow, W. J., & Laviolette, S. R. (2019). Cannabidiol Counteracts the Psychotropic Side-Effects of Δ-9-Tetrahydrocannabinol in the Ventral Hippocampus through Bidirectional Control of ERK1-2 Phosphorylation. The Journal of neuroscience : the official journal of the Society for Neuroscience, 39(44), 8762–8777. https://doi.org/10.1523/JNEUROSCI.0708-19.2019

Lee, Martin A. (2021) https://www.projectcbd.org/hub/science

Terpenes und Flavonoids

Baron, EP. (2018) Medicinal Properties of Cannabinoids, Terpenes, and Flavonoids in Cannabis, and Benefits in Migraine, Headache, and Pain: An Update on Current Evidence and Cannabis Science. Headache. 2018 Jul; 58(7):1139-1186. Doi: 10.1111/head.13345

Dosing and Methods of Consumption

Abrams, DI, Vizoso, HP, Shade SB, Jay, C. et al. (2007) Vaporization as a Smokeless Cannabis Delivery System: A Pilot Study. Clin Pharmacol Ther. 82•.572-578. doi: 10.1038/sj.clpt.6100200

Azorlosa, JL, Greenwald, MK, Stitzer, ML. (1995) Marijuana smoking: effects of varying puff volume and breathhold duration. J Pharmacol Exp Ther. 272(2):560-9. PMID: 7853169

St. Laurent, J, Goodrich, Scott. (2004) Cannabis vaporizer combines efficient delivery of THC with effective suppression of pyrolytic compounds. J Cannabis Therapeutics. 4:7-27. doi: 10.1300/J175v04n01_02.

MacCallum, Caroline A., Russo, Ethan Budd (2018) Practical considerations in medical cannabis administration and dosing. Eur J Intern Med. doi: 10.1016/j.ejim.2018.01.004

Experiential Reports about the Cannabis High

Grinspoon, Lester (1971) Marihuana Reconsidered. Cambridge, M.A. Harvard University Press.

Grinspoon, Lester (Hg.) (2021) www.marijuana-uses.com.

Lludlow, Fitz Hugh, (1857/1979) The hasheesh eater: Being passages from the life of a Pythagorean City Lights Books; First Edition

Michaux, Henri (1953) Miserable Miracle. Translated by Varese, L., San Francisco: City Lights Books.

Novak, William (1980) High Culture: Marijuana in the Lives of Americans. Massachusetts: The Cannabis Institute of America, Inc.

Solomon, David (ed.) (1966) The Marihuana Papers. New York: Signet Books.

The Mind-Enhancing Potential of Cannabis

Dolce, Joe (2016) Brave New Weed, HarperCollins Publishers, New York.

Gold, Shawn (2021) Creative Thinking Journal, pilgrmsoul. com /journals

Marincolo, Sebastián (2021) *www.marijuana-insights.com*

Marincolo, Sebastián (2015) What Hashish Did To Walther Benjamin, Khargala Press, Stuttgart.

Marincolo, Sebastián (2010) High. Insights on Marijuana. Indianapolis, Minneapolis.

Novak, William (1987) High Culture: Marijuana in the Lives of Americans. American Institute for Mindfulness.

Sagan, Carl (1971) "Mr. X", in Marihuana Reconsidered, Grinspoon, Lester Cambridge, Massachusetts, Harvard University Press.

Silva, Jason (2021) www.youtube.com/user/shotsofawe

Tart, Charles T. (1971) On Being Stoned: A Psychological Study of Marijuana Intoxication. Palo Alto, Cal.: Science and Behavior Books.

Altered States of Consciousness

Tart, Charles T. (ed.) (1969) Altered States of Consciousness. John Wiley and Sons.

Schmidt, Timo T., Berkemeyer, Hendrik (2018) The Altered States Database: Psychometric Data of Altered States of Consciousness, Frontiers in Psychology, Volume 9, DOI:10.3389/fpsyg.2018.01028

Cannabis und Music

Fachner, Jörg (2008) An Ethno-Methodological Approach to Cannabis and Music Perception, with EEG Brain Mapping in a Naturalistic Setting, Anthropology of Consciousness, January 8 2008, https://doi.org/10.1525/ac.2006.17.2.78

Famous Cannabis Users

Ellen Komp (2021) *www.veryimportantpotheads.com*

Risks

Nutt, David (2021) https://www.drugscience.org.uk/

Medical Cannabis

Health Canada (2021) https://www.canada.ca/en/health-canada/topics/cannabis-for-medical-purposes.html

Grotenhermen, Franjo (2020) Cannabis Healing: A Guide to the Therapeutic Use of CBD, THC, and Other Cannabinoids. Park Street Press.

About The Author

Sebastián Marincolo aka Dr. Sebastian Schulz studied philosophy and linguistics at the University of Tübingen and at the UNC at Chapel Hill in the USA. He was a student of philosophers Manfred Frank, Gianfranco Soldati, Dorit Bar-On, William Lycan, and Simon Blackburn. His research focuses on human and artificial consciousness and altered states of consciousness.

Harvard Medical School Assoc. Prof. of Psychiatry Emeritus Lester Grinspoon was a longtime friend and mentor for his research. Marincolo has published four books and numerous essays on the cannabis high. His work has received international recognition and has been covered in many media outlets, including SPIEGEL-Online, the 3sat/ZDF TV-magazine *kulturzeit*, Aidan McCullen's *The Innovation Show,* and Joe Dolce's *Brave New Weed* podcast. The cannabis advocate Gregory Frye published an Ebook on his work in 2021. Marincolo currently lives with his family near Frankfurt on the Main and works as an author, researcher and consultant.

Homepage

sebastianmarincolo.de

Blog

marijuana-insights.com